SIX PACK ABS IN 90 DAYS

Tarun Gill

Invincible Publishers

First published in India in 2019

ISBN : 978-93-88333-58-0

Invincible Publishers

Registered Address: 201A, SAS Tower, Sector 38, Gurgaon-122003

Printed in India by Excel Printers Pvt. Ltd.

The information in this book is meant to supplement, not replace, proper (name your sport) training. Like any sport involving speed, equipment, balance and environmental factors, (this sport) poses some inherent risk. The authors and publisher advise readers to take full responsibility for their safety and know their limits. Before practicing the skills described in this book, be sure that your equipment is well maintained, and do not take risks beyond your level of experience, aptitude, training, and comfort level. (sports, training)

Dedicated to my father

Joginder Gill

Acknowledgement

Want to thank so many people who made this book happen.

My mother, who has been my support system

My wife, who supported me throughout in my fitness journey

My mentor, Aditya Ghosh, who believed in me, when no one else did.

My mentor and friend, Puneet Nindra for his constant support.

My Friend, Amit Yadav, who got me in the fitness industry

Each one has a role to play and I would not have been here without them.

SATNAM VAHEGURU

SIX PACK

IN 90 DAYS

Believe it or not, six-pack these days has become the gold standard of fitness. If you have those rippling six-pack abs you are considered to be super fit. Did you know six-pack is also one of the most searched keyword in the online fitness world? Which tells you that how obsessed our generation is for six-pack.

Films and actors have a lot to do with spreading this rage as wild fire. Who can forget Hrithik Roshan in Dhoom2, or Aamir Khan in Ghajini, who took aesthetics to a totally different level! With Salman Khan introducing the concept of beautiful muscles in Bollywood, the six-pack era took off from there.

Everyone from a fifteen-year-old schoolboy to a fifty-year-old man has now found a new fitness goal. A goal to look aesthetic with shredded six pack abs!? Now that's established that everyone wants six pack abs, but the real questions are-

- Is it possible for anyone to get these six packs
- How long will it take to get those abs
- Is there a specific age that people can get these abs
- Is there a special training for them
- Is there a special diet
- Do we have to take any supplements

What is it that one has to do to get six-pack?

All these questions will now get answered, that is why I wrote this book in the first place.

Lets get started

You already have abs

If I were to tell you that you already have six pack abs as you read this book, would you believe me? Yes you heard it right. We all are born with six pack abs, its just the layer of fat which covers it making it impossible for anyone to see it with the naked eye.

That's a relief, right? You have six pack already, yippe!

Now that you know that you already have six pack, we need to address the bigger question.

How do we eliminate or minimize the layer of fat covering them.

I would not like to complicate this and make it extremely simple for you. If I were to tell you that you can minimize this fat layer and make your abs pop out in just 90 days, what would be your response?

Yes! You can get the abs in 90 days. But there are some conditions and stipulations.

- You need to be disciplined
- You cant cheat on your diet

- You cant cheat on your work out
- You need to commit to this goal for next 90 days

Now that you are aligned on these guidelines, lets start the journey.

What are six packs

Before we start what six packs are, lets understand the anatomy of it. Believe me I wont get technical about it.

Abs, called the rectus abdomen is muscle is a paired muscle running vertically on each side of the anterior wall of our abdomen. When you are talking about developing your six packs, you technically want to develop your rectus abdomen muscle.

For example if you say, I want to have bigger thighs; the thighs would be called the quadriceps, in scientific terms. I strongly feel you should know these

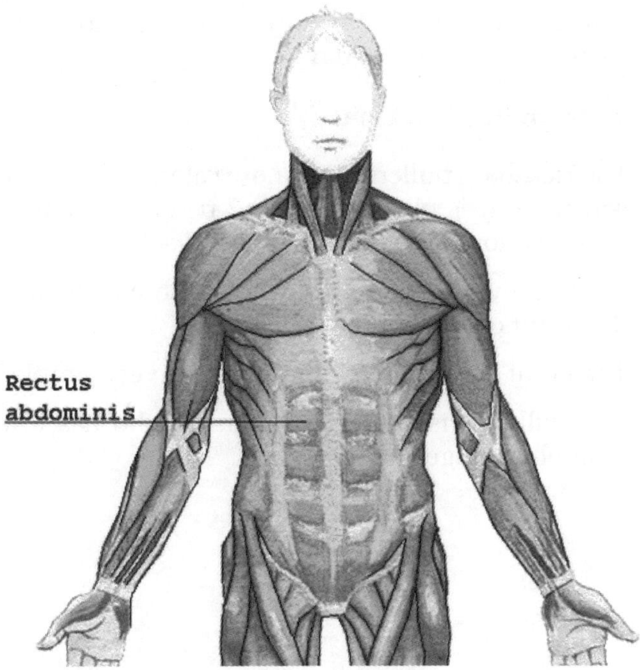

basic terms, because we are about to start our journey to build strong, solid core of our body, which would include our abdomen muscles.

Can anyone develop six pack abs

As I said earlier, we all are born with abs. You already have them, the effort is just to make them visible.

Don't believe me, just look at a labourer or a rickshaw puller. They are insanely shredded and have rippling abs. And they probably have never ever stepped a foot inside a gym let alone tried any abs exercise such as crunches or leg raises.

Did you ever wonder why their abs are so visible compared to someone who works out for six to seven days a week, two hours a day?

There are multiple reasons

- The rickshaw pullers burn more calories than they consume. It is obvious, pulling people for ten to fourteen hours is a tedious physical activity.
- Genetically, they may be lean. Which means they don't put on weight that easily.

The point I am trying to make here is very simple.

Abs will be visible for any person who has low body fat percentage.

"

I HAVE ABS. JUST HIDDEN UNDER MY LOVE FOR WINE

COSTES

Thousands of crunches every day

Now the first thing that will come into to your mind will be, "hey can I minimise my body fat by doing thousands of crunches?"

This is the mistake, ninety five percent people make. They think doing abs exercises for hours, will make their abs visible. Let me burst the bubble.

Doing abs exercises for hours will not get you six pack abs.

Do you think doing biceps exercise for hours will make your arms grow. Absolutely not!

The only way your abs will show if you follow a proper diet and training routine. Haven't you heard that saying.

"Abs are made in the gym but revealed in the kitchen". Now the question is where do you find this kitchen. This is the kitchen of your own house.

So stop doing crunches and abs exercises, they would not be of any help if your body fat is over eighteen percent.

I am too old or too young to get abs

Abs is not my thing! Let me tell you, abs is everyone's thing. Deep down we all want those abs. when we say it is not our thing, we are only implying that we either don't know how to get them or have failed in the past to get them.

We are never too old or too young for six-pack abs. We always want them. What we need is direction and guidance to equip us with the necessary tools to get there. And this is what this manual will do for you- Your abs mentor.

Not to forget, it eventually boils down our commitment and discipline and most importantly our desperation and hunger to get the abs.

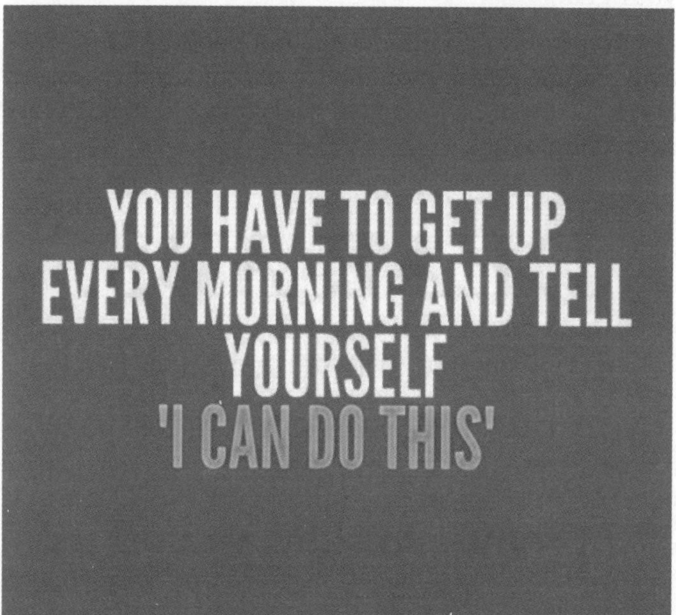

I am impatient–How long will it take

So how long does it take for anyone to get six pack abs? I wish I could put a definite timeline around it but I wont. Here is why.

We all are born different with different body types and genetic makeover. What may work on some people may not work on others. There is no vanilla program but a blueprint, which you can customize as per your body and how it will respond.

The program in this book has worked on many people with basic tweaks. Some people have gotten results in eight weeks where as some had to wait for sixteen weeks for it to kick in. It entirely depends on you, how you stay focused and determined to get to your goal.

Rome wasn't built in a day but people had to work every single day to build it. Same thing applies to your body. You will have to give everything to it and work every single day.

DEAR ABS:

I may not see you, but I feel you brewing something serious. Can't wait to finally meet you! I promise to show you off as often as I can!!

It is more mental than physical

The training program in this manual is challenging to a certain degree, but I am sure you can pull it off. On the contrary, training will be the easy part, food is where you would be tested.

Think about it, training would only constitute forty-five minutes to one hour a day. But the remaining twenty-three hours is where you would find yourself fighting. You heard me right: fighting. Fighting with yourself. These twenty-three hours will test your mettle. Whether you give into temptation or stick to your guns.

Fighting temptation

Even though we say, we want six packs, but deep down we are not convinced that we can actually get them. So the biggest fight we are fighting is with ourselves. And that is why we fail in our goal. But the day you convince yourself that you truly deserve to be the best version of yourself, getting six packs will become a walk in the park.

So here is what you should do to convince yourself

See how you would look in those abs. That picture, which you have painted in your mind, need to be manifested. Go to google. And then find a similar picture, which you have envisioned in your mind of your dream body.

Next thing, take multiple print outs of that picture and put in key locations of your house. Starting with kitchen. Because this picture, will be your weapon, which will protect you from temptation. The moment you feel like giving in this temptation, look at that picture and ask yourself

Do I really need to eat it. If I do, will it delay my goal! And you will get an instant answer.

Common mistakes you are making

Obviously you have been asking yourself, that I have done all the right things, trained for hours, starved for days, why isn't do I have six packs. I thought that's what it takes to be shredded.

Wrong!

You have been doing all the wrong things. You don't have to train for long and definitely don't have to starve yourself. I am listing few things, which you need to now change immediately.

Not knowing your body fat percentage

Let me ask you this – do you know your current body fat percentage. I am not asking about your weight. I am asking how much your total body fat percentage is right now.

IDEAL BODY FAT PERCENTAGE CHART (American Council on Exercise)		
Description	**Men**	**Women**
Essential fat	2-5%	10-13%
Athletes	6-13%	14-20%
Fitness	14-17%	21-24%
Average	18-24%	25-31%
Obese	25%+	32%+

Do you know

For your abs to be visible, you need to be in the body fat percentage bracket of 6-13%. Depending on your body type, a normal average person would be in 18-24%. You need to go from 18 to 10% for your six pack abs.

IDEAL BODY FAT PERCENTAGE CHART
(Jackson & Pollock)

Age (Years)	Body Fat %	
	Men	Women
20	8.5%	17.7%
25	10.5%	18.4%
30	12.7%	19.3%
35	13.7%	21.5%
40	15.3%	22.2%
45	16.4%	22.9%
50	18.9%	25.2%
55	20.9%	26.3%

References:
Jackson AS, Pollock ML. Generalized equations for predicting body density of men. Br J Nutr. 1978;40(3):497-504.
Jackson AS, Pollock ML, Ward A. Generalized equations for predicting body density of women. Med Sci Sports Exerc. 1980;12(3):175-81.

Not knowing your body type

As mentioned earlier, most of the people don't even know their body type. Here is a look at your body type.

- **Ectomorph-** If you are genetically skinny, and don't put on weight or muscle easily. Because they are genetically skinny and lean, their body fat percentage is low and will not have a tough time getting their six packs. They have a super fast metabolism, which helps them burn food faster than a Ferrari. Example Ranbir kapoor, Rajkumar Rao, Sushant Singh Rajput.

- **Mesomorph-** Genetically blessed with considerable amount of muscle mass. They have everything and with minimal effort they can get their six packs. They also have a reasonably fat metabolism. Example John Abraham, Tiger Shroff
- **Endomorph-** Prone to put on and lose weight easily. Most of the Indian men fall into this category. They have a very lethargic and slow metabolism which prevents them from having those abs. Example Govinda, Anil kapoor

You can also be a blend of two body types

Knowing your body type should always be a first step in your six pack journey. Basis that you can visualize a goal for your body!

WORD OF ADVICE

If you are an endomorph, don't set an unrealistic goal to go extremely skinny like an ectomorph. Though you may achieve that goal but it will be very short lived. The moment you exceed your daily calorie intake for a few days, you will start to put on weight.

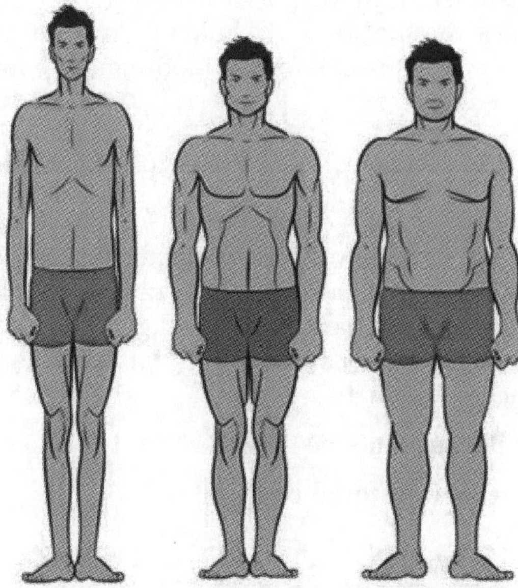

Know the difference

Fat loss vs Weight loss

People often confuse losing weight with losing fat. Let me share the difference.

Anyone can lose weight! Just don't eat for a few days, which is exactly what people do when they go on crash diets, starving themselves for days. What happens then is that they lose water weight along with some muscle mass. And the minute you start eating, the water weight comes right back. That is why people have a tough time maintaining consistent weight.

Remember the more muscle mass you have on your body, the lesser the body will hold fat. And weight loss itself as a process is making you loose muscle mass as well.

Weight loss = Muscle loss + Water loss + Fat loss

Fat loss on the other hand, focuses more on minimizing stored body fat percentage. You would find in our six pack journey that your weight may not change but your fat percentage will go down. Always as a thumb rule, check your body fat percentage not how much you weigh.

Don't believe me see this

Fat loss = Losing stored body fat

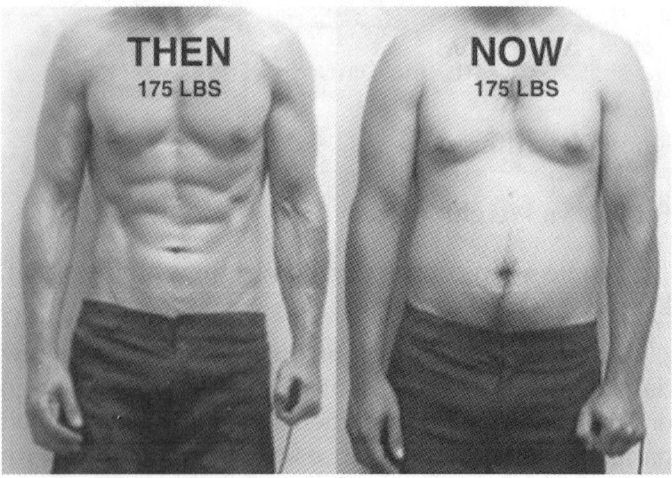

Know your metabolism

It surprises me when I see so many young men training for years, don't really know what their body metabolism is!

Well first let me explain what metabolism is. And I will try to make it so simple for you that it becomes extremely easy for you to identify the speed of your metabolism

What is metabolism ?

Metabolism is our body's ability to convert food into energy. What you eat and drink during the day, how fast or slow your body utilizes that food into energy. The faster your metabolism, more easy you lose fat. The slower your metabolism, the difficult it gets for you to lose fat.

Remember, body is a complex machinery. It is using energy for everything even when you breathe, walk, move hands or any function both internal and external.

In our six pack journey, it is important to keep your metabolism at good pace, and don't let it slow down. Yes we can manipulate our metabolism to a certain degree. This way you keep burning more calories.

All about calories

I am sure you must have heard this from so many guys!

- Dude how many calories do you take in a day?
- What are your macros (the latest buzzword in fitness)

Surprisingly, people who ask such questions don't even know what calories are in the first place.

What is a calorie?

A calorie is a unit of energy, which in nutrition refers to energy we get from eating any kind of food. Calories are what you would find on every food label. This is how you calculate how much you have to eat on a daily basis to get six packs.

Calories are important, but more important is the source/substance where those calories are coming from.

And we only have three substances/sources

which are also called macro nutrients

- **Protein**
- **Carbohydrates**
- **Fats**

For your understanding, you just need to remember this

- **1 gram of protein contains 4 kcal**
- **1 gram of carbohydrates contains 4 kcal**
- **1 gram of Fats contains 9 kcal**

That's all you need to know, so you could calculate how many calories you need on a daily basis.

For example if you now read the label which says protein 15 grams then what you would do is apply the formula

15 grams protein * 4 = 60 calories

And you can apply the same for other macros too

Now the question is how do you know how many calories do you need to consume every day for six packs.

Here I would suggest you follow a simple formula which is easily available online free of cost called Total daily energy expenditure (TDEE)

TDEE formula captures your inputs including age, height, weight and lifestyle and tells you the number of calories you need everyday to function.

Calorie deficit

Now that you have calculated your TDEE, you need to remember, that to get six packs, which is to minimize body fat, we need to create a calorie deficit.

How do you create a calorie deficit ?

Create a calorie deficit by eating less and burning more. For example, if your TDEE is 2500 calories, you now need to eat less than 2500 to create a calorie deficit. This way you will be able to burn fat at a much effective pace.

In simple terms

Eat less than you are required to. But don't cut down your calories drastically. Which most people do. That way you will not be able to sustain the fat loss.

Sleep is your friend

You have captured your TDEE, you have two options to create a deficit

- Eat less calories
- Or Burn more calories

So what is that one activity that we do daily which burns the maximum amount of calories. Nope, it's not training.

An eight-hour sleep burns maximum calories for your body. This is why sleep and recovery will play a key role in our six-pack journey.

This is one of the reason you can't compromise your eight hours beauty sleep because this is where you are burning maximum calories. And not having a sound eight-hour sleep raises our body cortisol levels, the stress hormone which only attacks the abdomen fat.

So if you have been wondering why you have not been successful in getting your six-pack despite your great training and diet routine. Well lack of sound sleep could be a reason.

Plus a great sleep also raises your body natural testosterone levels which plays a key role in adding that quality muscle mass to our frame. More muscle means lesser fat and lesser fat deposits means visible abs.

Exercise can't make up for bad diet

Now this is one of the single largest reasons why people fail in their six pack abs quest. They feel that when they exercise six days a week for consecutive hours, they can get away with eating junk.

Let me break it for you! Exercise and training cant make up for a bad diet. If your diet is not on point, but you are training religiously, you are only compromising on your results.

Haven't you heard " I can eat anything because I have trained for two hours in the gym today". By eating anything you have just equalized those two hours or rather wasted those hours.

Remember its not just the training, good food is the backbone of six pack abs. it does matter where the calories come from.

It's a lifestyle

People think that once they get their abs, they will get back to their usual not so healthy habits of eating anything and everything. Remember, six pack abs is a lifestyle, and you have to sign up for this lifestyle for the rest of your life. Only if you want to see your abs for the rest of your life!

It is not shortcut or make arrangement for a vacation or a Goa trip. It is something you have to live and breathe. Only if you are ready then you should follow the plan.

Let the journey begin

Cleaning up the kitchen

This is where it starts. When it comes to getting a dream body, we usually start our journey with finding a right gym. Which I believe is not the right approach. As I mentioned earlier, you would only be spending forty to sixty minutes in the gym that too five to six days a week.

Your ideal focus should be the kitchen. This is where it starts.

What you eat during the day will decide the results you will see in the next couple of weeks. So it is pivotal for you to start cleaning up your kitchen and remove all the junk from it.

What you have to remove

Breads and pizzas- trust me you think one slice wont make a difference but one slice every now and then will become a full eight-piece pizza in no time.

Beverages – Sodas, canned juices are loaded with sugar. Even a small serving of such drinks can spike up your insulin levels, which will make you crave for more sugar. And your cravings will put an end to your diet and your goal.

Milk – Now you would feel that why am I asking you to remove milk from your diet. Well there is a good reason for that. Not because most of the people are lactose intolerant but because of milk sugar, which hits your belly fat. Now you would say that you have a habit of having milk everyday with breakfast or before going off to sleep. Too bad! You may have to change it now.

Alcohol – I know you want to party every weekend because you work extremely hard through the week. Partying means alcohol and some social drinking at home with friends over. Socializing with friends is not a problem but drinking is.

Because it is never usually one drink, it carries on till it hits us. And even if you have limited drinks, you would also want to munch on salty snacks. So here goes your diet plan. Plus not to forget the hangover the following morning! You will surely miss your work out.

Fast food – I always had the habit of eating food on the go. And therefore junk food topped my list. But we all know why junk food is called junk food. It is loaded with carbs, especially white bread, adding unnecessary calories to your Total daily energy expenditure (TDEE)

Prepare your food

Now that you have cleaned up your kitchen, it is important for you to develop a habit of preparing your own meals. I am not implying that you become a master chef. But only if you cook, you will be in control of what you put inside your body. Rather someone else telling you the ingredients.

It would be tough initially but the food items you will be preparing are so easy to make that you would start enjoying cooking after preparing few initial meals.

But to start with, whosoever is cooking for you, you would have to shadow that person and tell him/her to cook as per the meal plan I share with you.

All our meals will have

- Limited salt
- Limited oil
- Minimal cooking

You would be eating grilled or sauted food and meat (as your daily protein). Cooking sauted food only requires you to put all the food items on the pan and sauté them for ten to fifteen minutes.

And most importantly, if you are a working professional, you would have to carry all your meals everyday to work or college. No college canteen food to office cafeteria meals. Remember you are not dependent on anyone, you not only know your meals but also carry your meals. This discipline is one of the most effective ways to get six pack.

Most of the people don't want to put in the effort. Grilled chicken has very different ingredients at restaurants compare to what you would cook at home. Restaurant food is made for taste but our food is made for results.

Eat for results not taste

Now this brings me to taste. If you are serious about results, please let go of the taste. People with great physique and six packs have forgotten how spices taste like.

Remember you have to eat for results not for taste. And this is exactly what I had shared in my previous section. Six pack journey, is a lifestyle change. To achieve not so normal results you have to do things, which are not so normal.

You would now be eating for nutrition. Food, which will help you grow your body and minimize your body fat. The goal is to get results with your food. Earlier you were burning bad food choices in the gym now, you would be reaping good results in the gym for your healthy food choices.

This is the classic shift, which will not be easy to get used to! I am warning you, the first week will be extremely difficult but if you survive this week, next twenty-five years you will live with the body of your choice.

Food will now be your friend, and will be working closely with your training program. Earlier it was working against your goal because of your bad food choices.

What exactly we would be eating will come in the next sections. But be prepared it wont be easy. Brace yourself.

Visualize

Visualizing is one of the most effective tools, which will help you get to your goal. Let me explain how the concept of visualization works.

- Visualize in your mind how you would want to look with six pack abs
- Remember, the goal starts with a thought then takes a shape of visualization

- Think of how you would feel when you get those six packs.
- Bombard your mind with positivity
- Think about how you will train
- And pep yourself every couple of hours, that you can do this.

Now you must be thinking, do I have to talk to myself? The answer is yes. You are constantly giving yourself a pep talk. Because what you are doing is motivating your mind to do it. The mind conceives and the body achieves.

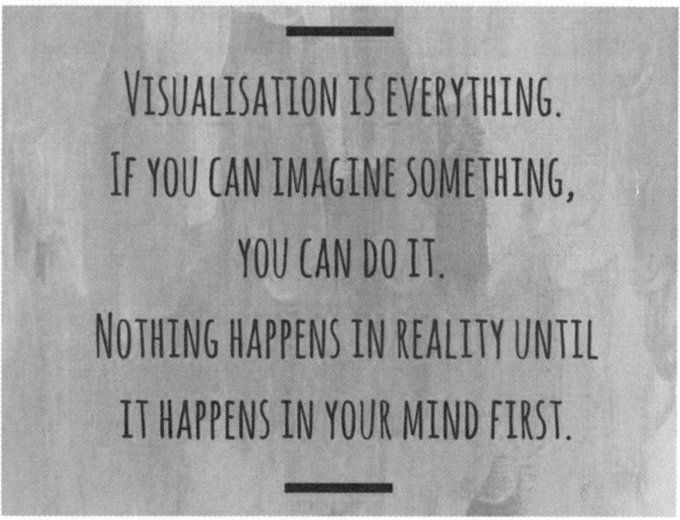

Train with a purpose

I presume you have been training for some time now. And also have not been too successful in your quest for six pack abs. I have shared many reasons for your failure. But this one could be the eye opener.

You have always approached training with an intention to get shredded or to get six pack abs. But you never really thought why am I training, what is my purpose.

Remember purpose gives perspective, it answers your "why" which is why are you training for six pack abs in the first place. If you have a purpose, you will always be motivated. You will never lose motivation. Because you will always have visibility to your goal!

So ask yourself! Why do I want six pack abs? The deeper the purpose the easier will be the process to get it.

For example, if you have had a heartbreak recently. Proving someone wrong who broke up with you could be a purpose in itself, so start thinking on these lines.

TRAIN WITH A PURPOSE. EAT WITH A PLAN.

SLICKWORDS.COM

Eat with a plan

As I shared above, your eating has to have a plan. Take this program like your biggest project; you will ever work on yourself. Now you cant just put anything in your body. You need to plan your everyday diet and most importantly stick to it.

Gone are the days, when you would indulge in an ice cream telling yourself, " one wont make a difference". Well guess what, it does make a difference.

In the following sections, I will be giving you the diet plan, which you have to follow for the next 90 days. There cannot be room for any deviations.

Now its time to bust out some myths! Before I share the plan with you, I want to bust out some myths around six pack abs. Everyone thinks there is a secret diet, a secret product, which people take to get their six pack.

These so called secret formulas have now become myths, which the world believes in. So lets bust them one by one.

THE BEST PROJECT YOU'LL EVER WORK ON IS YOU.

Myth # 1

No carbs if you want abs

This myth has been doing the rounds for over a decade now. People who are gunning for their six-pack abs have been told not to have carbohydrates (one of the macros which I discussed above). It's practically impossible for any human being to live without carbs in a diet.

Whatever you eat, it will have some carbs in it. Our brain only works on carbs. So technically you are depriving your brain from the food it needs to function properly. If your brain is not functioning at its optimal level, you can expect yourself to be cranky, irritated and depressed.

It you want to live like this for the rest of your life, that is entirely your call. But scientifically, you should not leave out carbs regardless of your goal. Remember carbs is not the enemy; it is the timing of carbs which prevents us from achieving our goals.

In our 90 days program, there will be certain amount of carbs, which we will add for you to function properly. And yea, you will have carbs in this program. But the quality of carbs is what I will guide you on.

Myth # 2

Lots of cardio for six-pack abs

I have seen so many people in the gym spending hours on the treadmill to get those six-pack abs. They pride themselves in telling people, on how much they ran. "I ran for one hour today, I burned fifteen hundred calories on a treadmill today". Sure you have heard of all that in your gym too.

But people who talk seldom get results. Little do they know that running for hours will not be of any help especially if your goal is to get six pack abs. If your goal is to be a marathon runner, than you can run for as long as you want to develop your endurance.

To get your six-pack, you don't have to run for hours. Your cardio sessions will be based on how many calories you consume on that particular day to create a maximum calories deficit.

The idea of cardio is to burn calories. you can burn calories by walking, cycling or even playing a sport for few minutes. But people have made cardio into a monster, which everyone seems to ignore.

In our program, we will be doing cardio but not for hours, only to maximize our calories deficit.

Myth # 3

Only supplements can get you six pack

We seriously think that there are some magical products, which we need to consume to get our six-pack abs. But the truth is, there is no magical product available in the world, which can guarantee six pack abs.

Whatever some companies claim, is not true. My only request is to stop believing all that you see on television. Especially, the infomercials, where one guy who goes fat to fab in one month by taking a product ! All those claims are not true at all, and you should never buy into that.

The only way to get six pack abs is a blend of training, clean diet, rest and basic supplementation. Remember what I just said. Basic supplementation.

Supplements, are meant to be supplemented with your diet not to be replaced. People often replace actual food with powders, which will not get you anywhere closer to your goal of six-pack abs.

Myth # 4

Training abs for hours will get you six-pack

This myth I am sure, even you have heard of. People doing crunches for hours thinking they are developing those six packs. The truth is doing thousands of abs, will not get you six-pack, they will only get stronger. As I have shared before, we need to focus on minimizing body fat. And doing abs exercises does not burn many calories.

On the contrary, you are only damaging your ab muscles by repeatedly doing abs.

Myth # 5

Training abs everyday will get you six pack

Not only people do endless ab exercises but they also perform these ab exercises every day. For them every day is an ab day. Haven't you seen people who after their work out, as a ritual and routine, go to ab board and do thousand of abs. From leg raises to crunches, they are unstoppable.

Remember just like any other muscle, ab is also a muscle group in our body. They need time to recover.

Doing them everyday will only fatigue them and prevent them to grow.

In this program we will not do abs everyday.

Myth # 6

Fats are bad for six-pack

I have made this mistake in the past of cutting out fats and carbs from my diet. Because of which my results were delayed.

The truth is, good fats can accelerate the fat loss process, paving a way for six packs to show. So whatever you do, do not cut out carbs and fat from your diet. Our 90 days diet will have a blend of everything.

Let the program begin

Training for six pack

Training for six-pack will be slightly different. Now this program is designed for someone who has been training for over three months. I am presuming you are comfortable going to the gym.

The training should not last for more than forty minutes to one hour. You don't want to burn yourself by overtraining. Overtraining will stop the growth and delay the process.

Also you should enjoy this process not just the end result. Remember it is not a torture, but you are now sculpting your body the way you would like to see.

We will be training six days a week in this program with a combination of both high intensity and steady state workouts with limited rest in between sets.

Bodyweight training

Before you hit the weight room, it is important for you to strengthen your base. And nothing builds the stronger foundation than bodyweight training. Bodyweight training is not a new concept; it is being used for years to deliver results.

Bodyweight training is any form of exercises, which involves your own bodyweight as resistance. Which means you don't have to go to the gym to lift weights, you can perform exercises anywhere using your own body weight.

Benefits of bodyweight training in six-pack

Fast gains

Bodyweight training is very efficient. You don't really have to spend more than thirty minutes to finish the workouts. And plus they yield amazing and fast results especially when it comes to minimizing body fat. This is because, the rest time in between sets is very limited, which keeps the heart rate very high in a fat burning zone.

Blend of cardio and strength

Most of the people fail in their training programs because they get bored following the same routine day in day out. The bodyweight training on the contrary keeps the work out very interesting. Bodyweight exercises are a blend of both strength and cardio, which can help you yield benefits of both forms of training. Not only you can lose fat but also build a strong foundation.

Complete work out

Body weight exercises are a complete work out. They engage all major muscle joints in every rep, resulting in the complete development of the muscles. And most the bodyweight exercises focuses on core strength, that is why it forms the basis for any six pack program.

Supplements

We have been told by many, that people with six pack abs have access to some magical products and supplements which has led to their chiseled washboard six packs. But no one actually tells us about those products and where to find them.

Before I break it down for you and disappoint you and tell you that there are no such products or supplements, which can get you the six-pack abs, I have to share something with you.

We have been living the lies for all these years.

- Companies claiming their pills work directly on the abs
- Brands promising their gel will melt the fat from the abs

Its time that someone should tell you the truth!

Abs are made with hard work, diet and training. Supplements and products do a role but very little. They play a role in fulfilling the requirement, which our natural diet can't! If your diet is on point, adding supplements will give your body the edge to perform at optimum level.

But what supplements do we really need to add.

I will add supplements in two categories.

- **Need to have**–Need to have are supplements which you must have in your six-pack arsenal.
- **Good to have**–Good to have are supplements, which you may help you in your journey for six-pack abs.

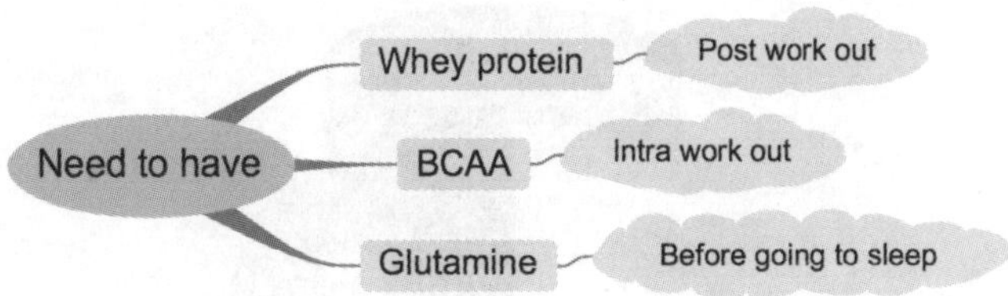

Need to have

Whey Protein

Some of you may have inhibitions consuming food supplements, thinking they are artificial powders, packed with chemicals and anabolics. But the truth is, some of the food supplements are natural and byproduct of dairy. Whey protein is one such product.

It has been scientifically proven that taking a scoop of whey protein after rigorous strength training helps our body to recover from the wear and tear of the muscles. Having said that, everyone reacts differently to whey protein. Exactly how you would react consuming any milk product! If milk doesn't suit your body, doesn't mean it is harmful for everyone.

Some people cannot digest milk, and get upset stomach drinking it. Similarly, first time consuming whey protein, may lead to some reactions. Once you take it, only then you would realize if it suits you or not. Remember, if it doesn't suit you doesn't mean it is harmful or has side effects.

BCAA–Branched chain amino acid

Without getting into the technicalities, all you need to know and why you need BCAA. Our body is complicated machinery, which is constantly processing food to give us the energy we need to perform our daily activities with ease.

There are over 20 amino acids, which our body needs. 9 out of 20 are considered to be essential amino acids, which typically means our body is not capable of making these aminos and we must obtain it from external sources through protein rich diet.

The supplement form of BCAA is made up of three essential amino acids.

- Leucine
- Isoleucine
- Valine

Why these three, because 35-40% of our body muscle protein is consist of the above amino acid profiles.

Just like whey protein, BCAAs also help us with recovery after a work out.

Glutamine

L glutamine is one amino acid, which our body produces naturally unlike BCAAs. But still I recommend L-glutamine because it has many benefits. Benefits, which has helped me in my journey of six-pack abs!

With intense training, our body cannot produce enough L-Glutamine, hence supplementing can help you recover faster from gruesome workouts.

Take 3-5 grams before going off to sleep.

Most of the supplements we are using in our six-pack journey will only help us with recovering faster from our workouts. Faster recovery will help us stay consistent with our training regime. And consistency will bring us closer to our goals.

Good to have supplements

These are the supplements you may need at times when you are not in the mood for a work out. That is why all of them fall in the category of pre workouts.

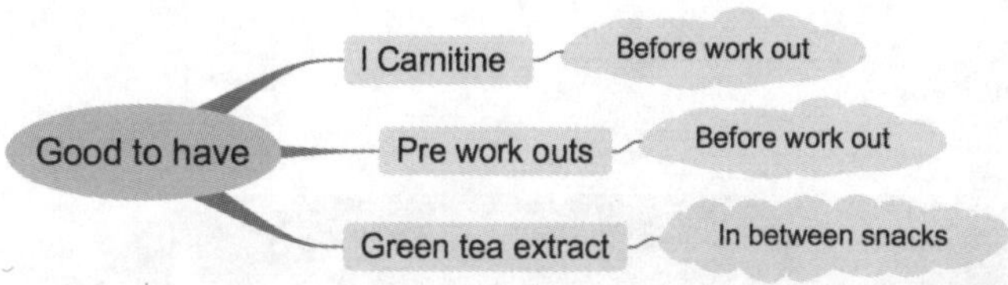

WEEK 1 AND 2

BODYWEIGHT TRAINING

Super set, with 25-second rest in between each exercise.

6 exercises makes one set, total we do 6 sets total 36 sets per workout on Monday, Wednesday and Friday.

MONDAY

EXERCISE # 1
PUSH UPS – 10 REPS

EXERCISE 2
FREE SQUATS- 10 REPS

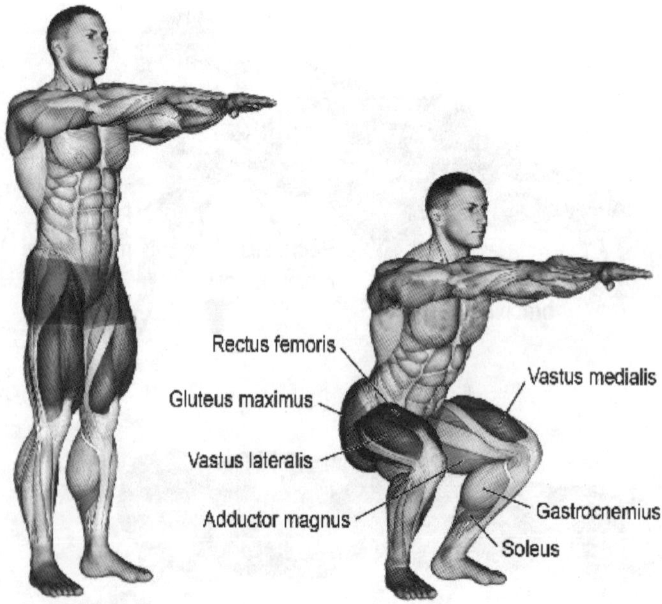

EXERCISE 3
JUMPING JACKS- 10 REPS

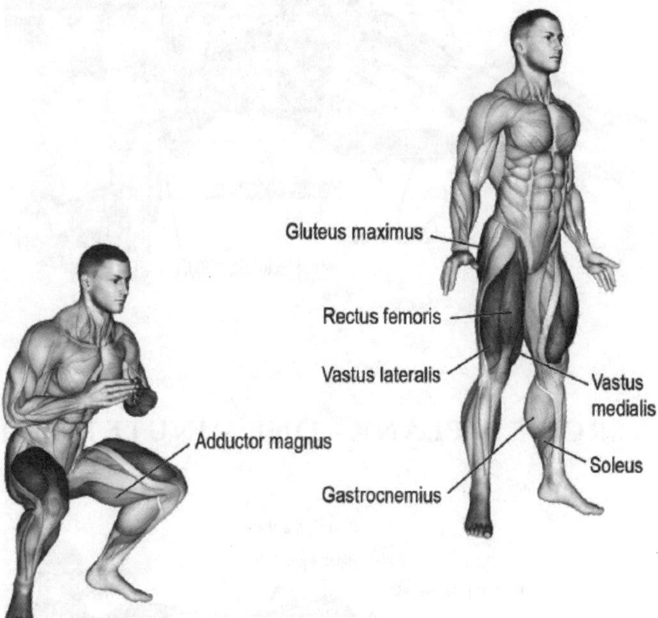

EXERCISE 4 - LUNGES- 10 REPS

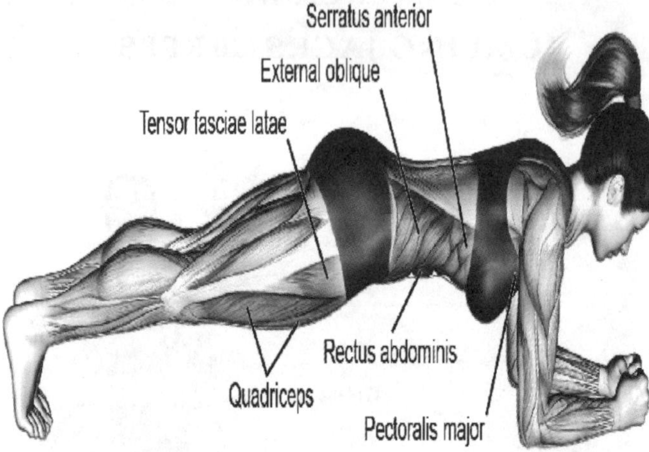

EXERCISE 5 - PLANK – ONE MINUTE HOLD

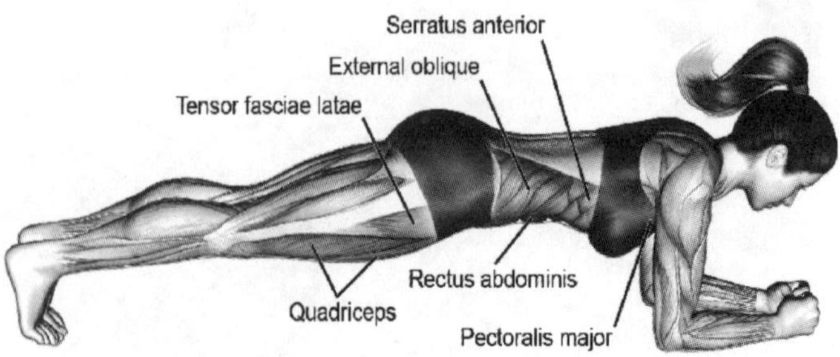

EXERCISE 6
PULL UPS – 10 REPS

WEDNESDAY AND FRIDAY

REPEAT MONDAY

WEEK 3 AND 4

STRENGTH TRAINING

Monday: Legs

Warm up

10 minutes walking

50 push ups (break it to a set of 3)

50 free squats

MAIN WORKOUT

LEG EXTENSION 4 SETS, 12 REPS EACH

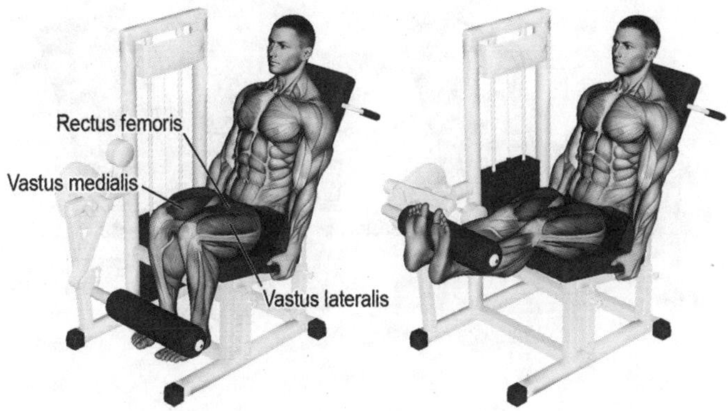

SQUATS (SMITH MACHINE) 4 SETS, 12 REPS EACH

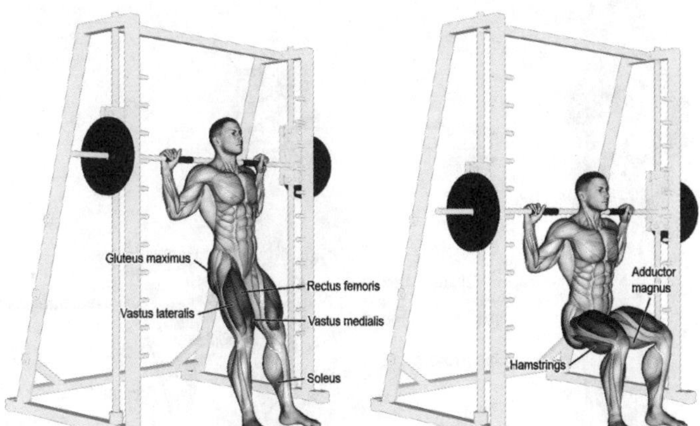

LEG CURL
4 SETS, 12 REPS EACH

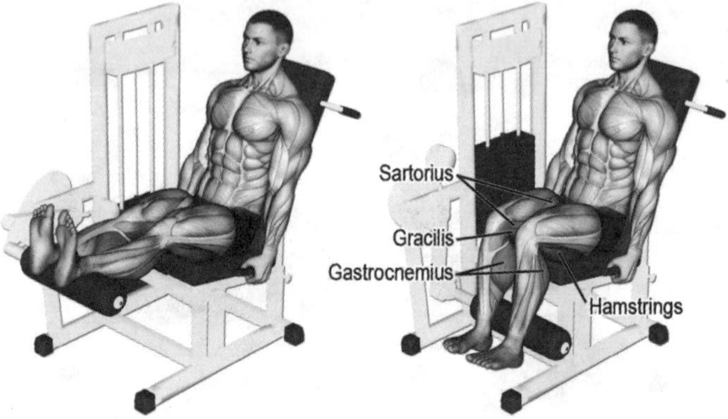

WALKING LUNGES
4 SETS, 12 REPS EACH

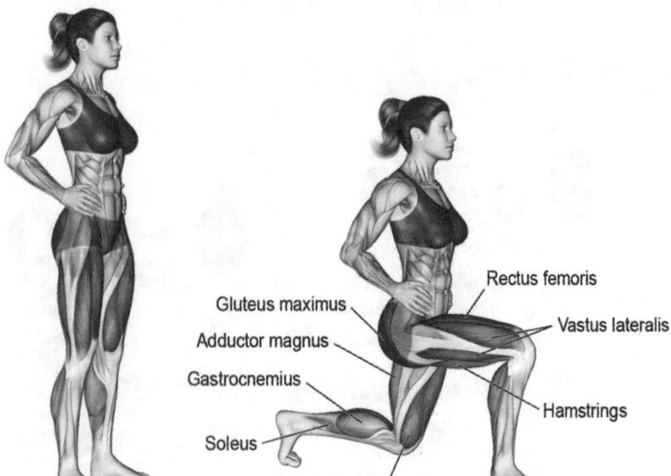

FREE SQUATS
6 SETS, 10 REPS EACH

CARDIO
20 MINUTES INCLINE
WALK ON TREADMILL

Tuesday: Chest and back

Warm up

10 minutes walking

50 push ups (break it to a set of 3)

MAIN WORKOUT CHEST

FLAT BENCH PRESS 4 SETS 12 REPS EACH

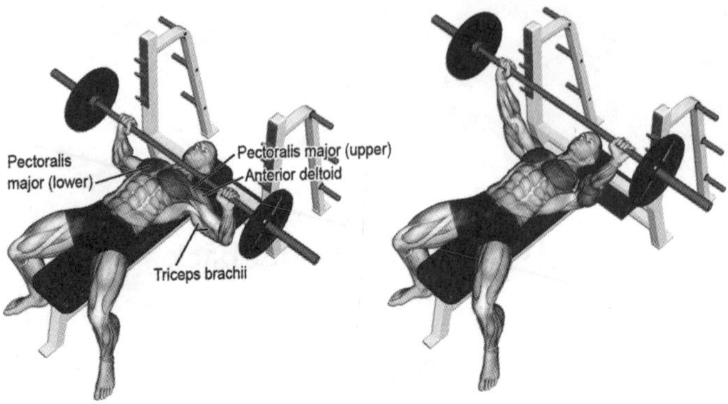

INCLINE DUMBELL PRESS 4 SETS 12 REPS EACH

FLAT FLYS 4 SETS 12 REPS EACH

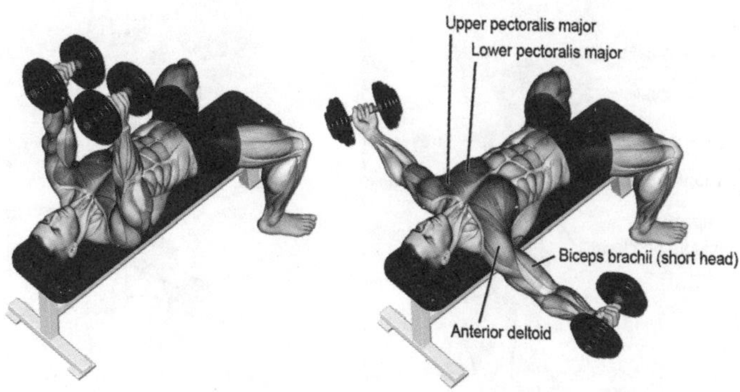

PEC DEC FLY
4 SETS 12 REPS EACH

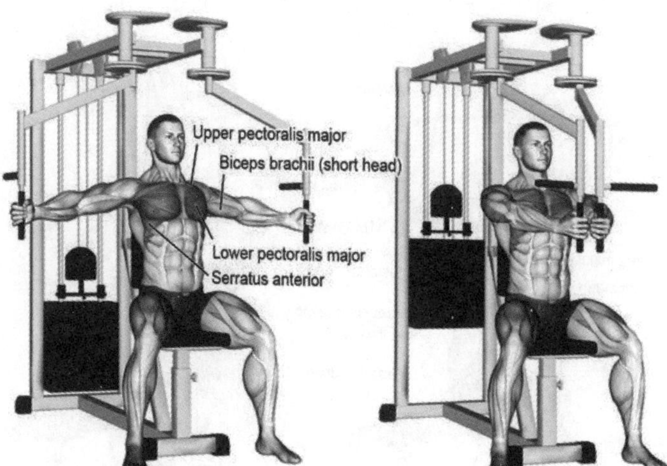

PULL UPS 4 SETS 12 REPS EACH

LAT PULL DOWN 4 SETS 12 REPS EACH

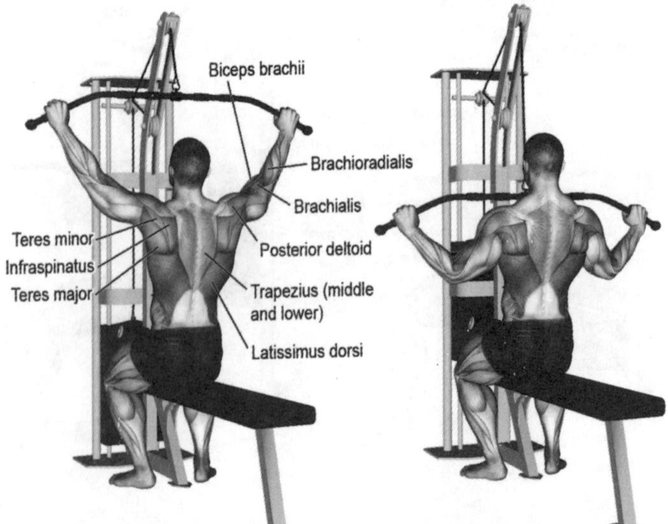

SINGLE ARM DUMBBELL ROW
4 SETS 12 REPS EACH

STANDING T BAR ROWS
4 SETS 12 REPS EACH

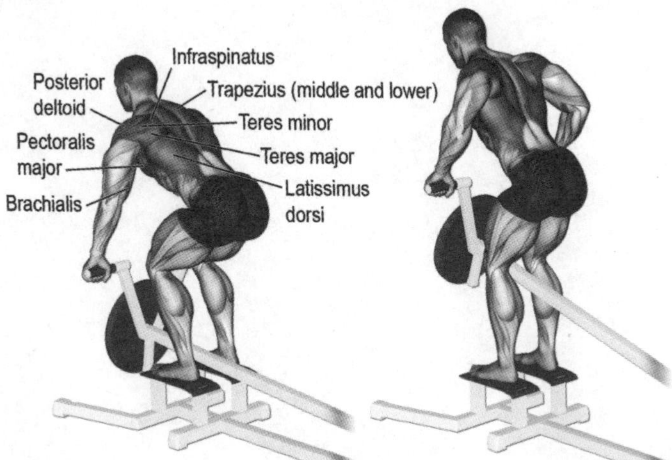

CARDIO
20 MINS INCLINE WALKING

Wednesday: Arms and abs

Warm up

10 minutes walking

50 push ups (break it to a set of 3)

MAIN WORKOUT ARMS

BARBELL CURLS
4 SETS 12 REPS EACH

TRICEP PUSH DOWN
4 SETS 12 REPS EACH

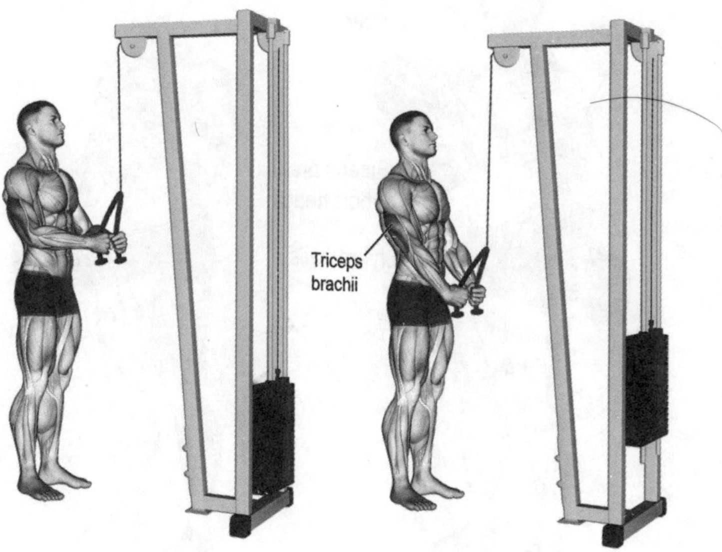

DUMBELL CURLS
4 SETS 12 REPS EACH

TRICEPS KICK BACKS
4 SETS 12 REPS EACH

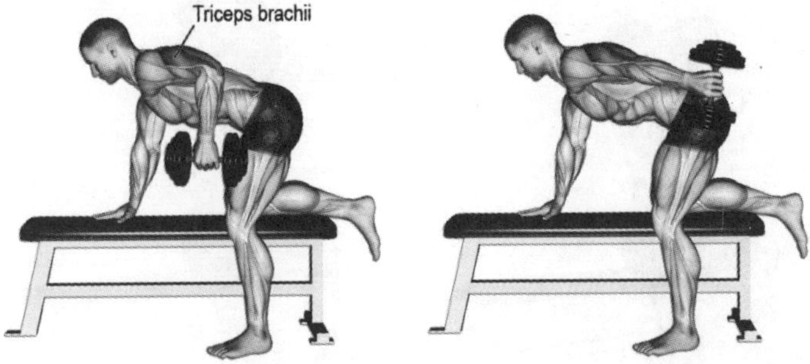

CONCENTRATION CURLS
4 SETS 12 REPS EACH

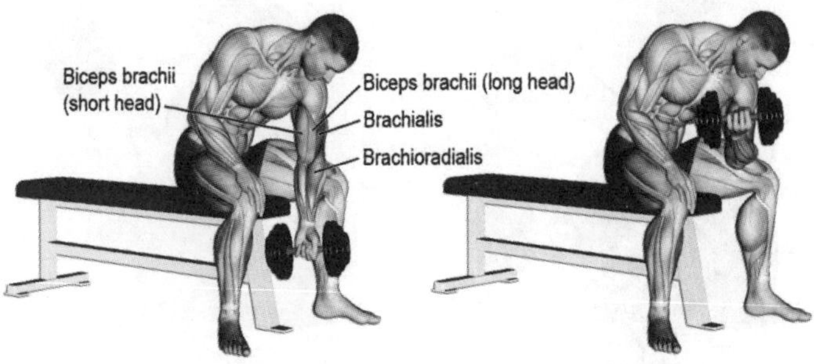

TRICEPS KICK BACKS
4 SETS 12 REPS EACH

PREACHER CURLS
4 SETS 12 REPS EACH

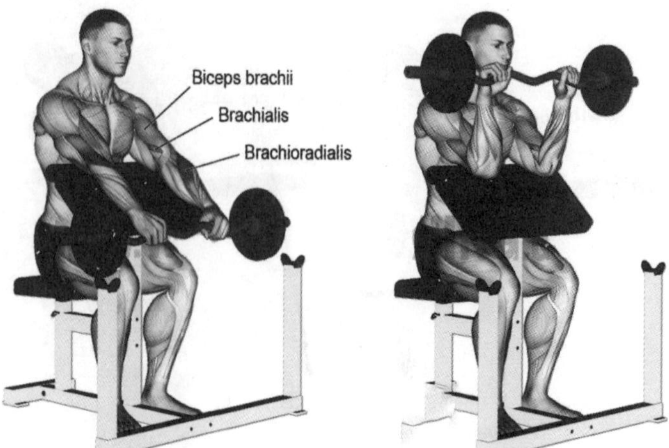

TRICEPS DIPS
4 SETS 12 REPS EACH

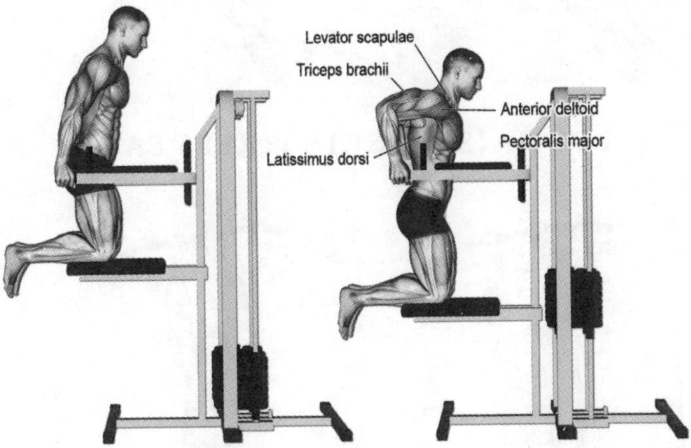

MAIN WORKOUT ABS

CRUNCHES 4 SETS 12 REPS EACH

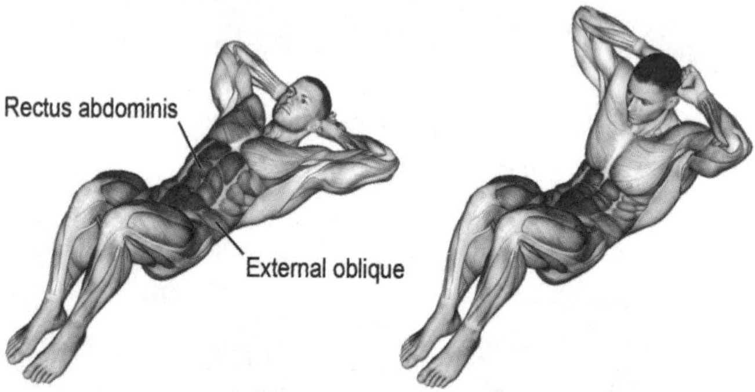

LEG RAISES 4 SETS 12 REPS EACH

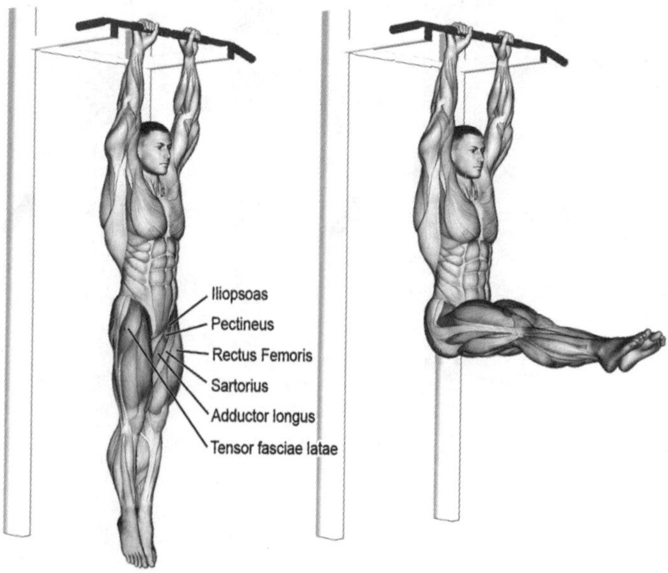

Thursday: Legs and shoulder

Warm up

10 minutes walking

50 push ups (break it to a set of 3)

50 free squats

MAIN WORKOUT LEGS

LEG EXTENSION 4 SETS, 12 REPS EACH

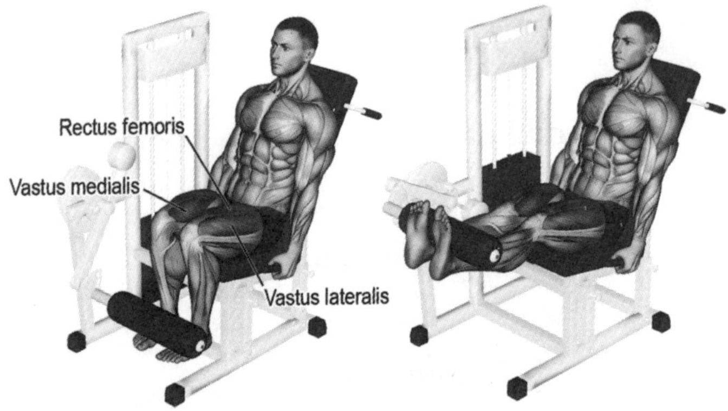

SQUATS 4 SETS, 12 REPS EACH

LEG CURL
4 SETS, 12 REPS EACH

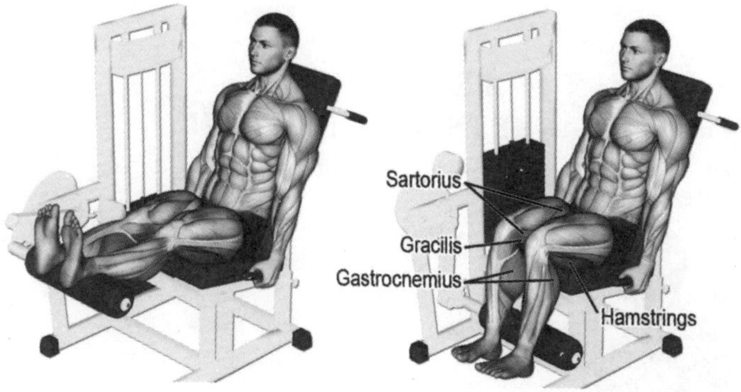

WALKING LUNGES
4 SETS, 12 REPS EACH

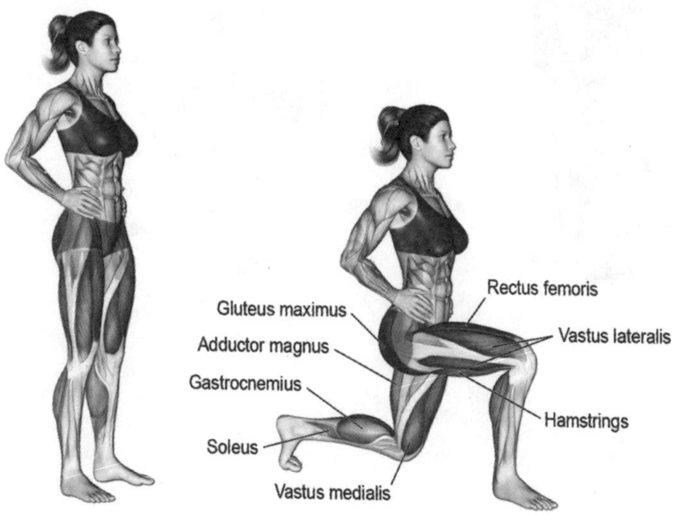

FREE SQUATS
6 SETS, 10 REPS EACH

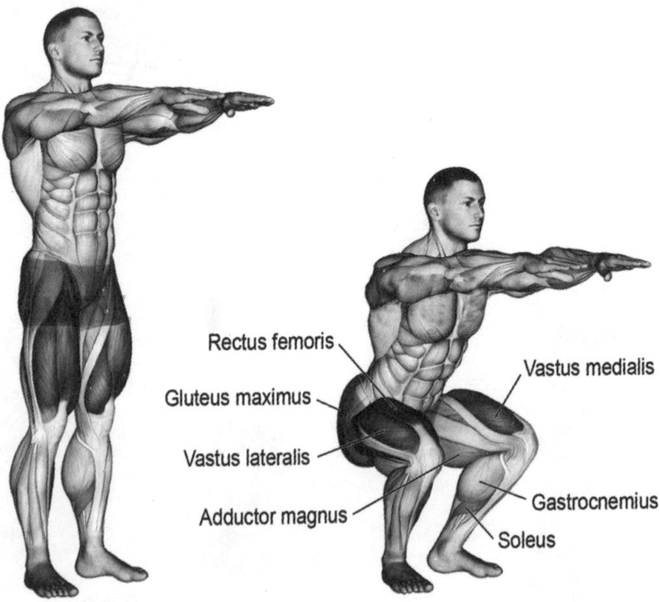

MAIN WORKOUT SHOULDERS

SHOULDER DUMBBELL PRESS
4 SETS, 12 REPS EACH

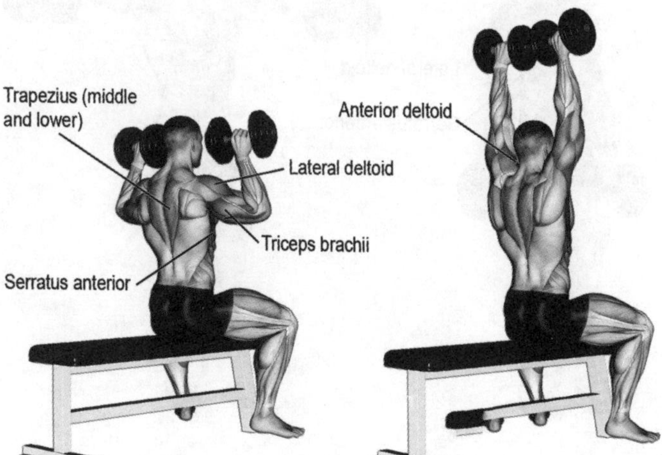

SIDE LATERALS
4 SETS, 12 REPS EACH

FRONT RAISES
4 SETS, 12 REPS EACH

SHRUGS
4 SETS, 12 REPS EACH

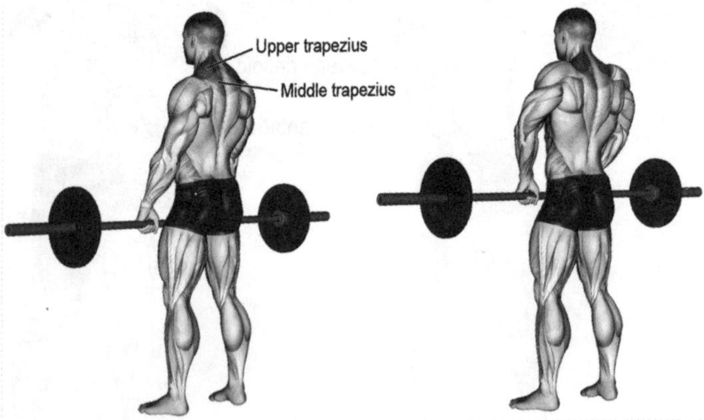

CARDIO
15 MINS WALKING

FRIDAY

REPEAT TUESDAY

SATURDAY

REPEAT WEDNESDAY

SUNDAY

REST

WEEK 5 AND 6

BRINGING IN VARIATION
PUSH AND PULL WORK OUTS

MONDAY

PUSH

WORKOUT

CHEST DUMBBELL PRESS
4 SETS, 12 REPS EACH

CHEST DUMBBELL FLY
4 SETS, 12 REPS EACH

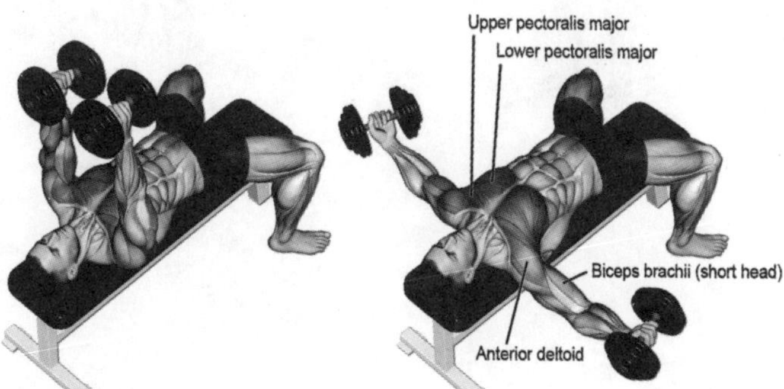

MILITARY BARBELL PRESS
4 SETS, 12 REPS EACH

SIDE LATERAL DUMBBELL RAISE
4 SETS, 12 REPS EACH

TRICEPS LYING EXTENSION
4 SETS, 12 REPS EACH

TRICEPS DUMBBELL EXTENSION
4 SETS, 12 REPS EACH

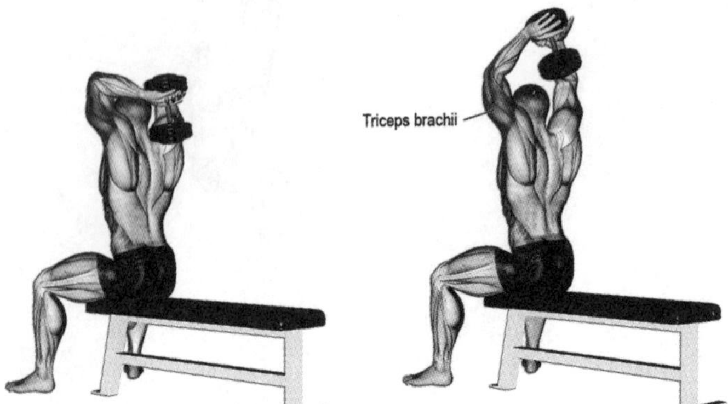

CARDIO

20 MINUTES

TUESDAY

PULL

WORKOUT

LAT PULL DOWN
4 SETS, 12 REPS EACH

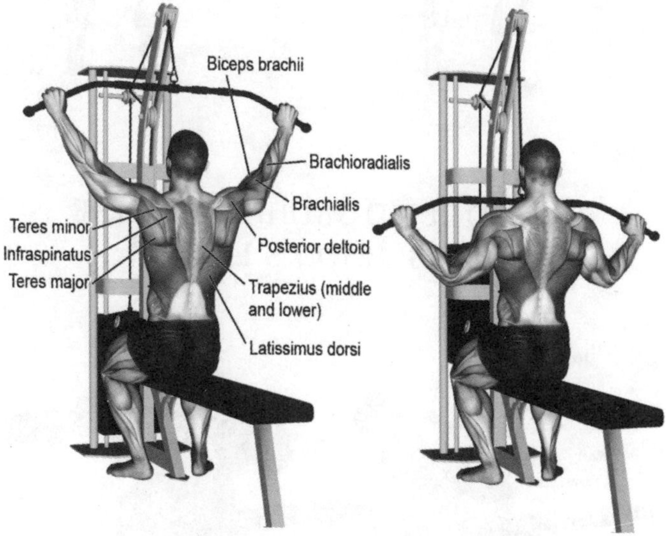

BARBELL BENT OVER ROW
4 SETS, 12 REPS EACH

REAR DELT DUMBBELL RAISE
4 SETS, 12 REPS EACH

LAT PULL DOWN
4 SETS, 12 REPS EACH

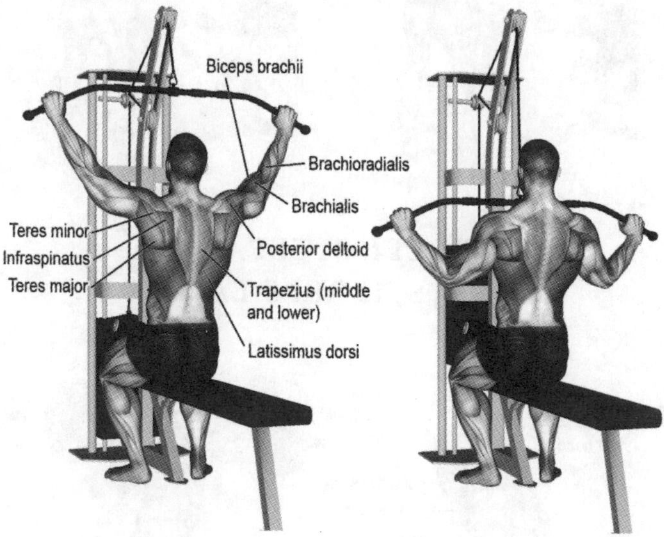

ROPE REAR DELT FACE PULL
4 SETS, 12 REPS EACH

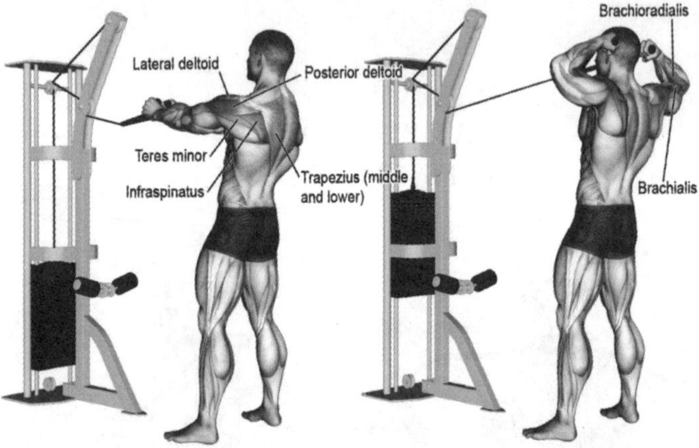

BARBELL BICEP CURL
4 SETS, 12 REPS EACH

DUMBBELL BICEP CURLS
4 SETS, 12 REPS EACH

CARDIO
15 MINUTES

WEDNESDAY

LEGS

BARBELL SQUATS
4 SETS, 12 REPS EACH

DUMBBELL STANDING LUNGE 4 SETS, 12 REPS EACH

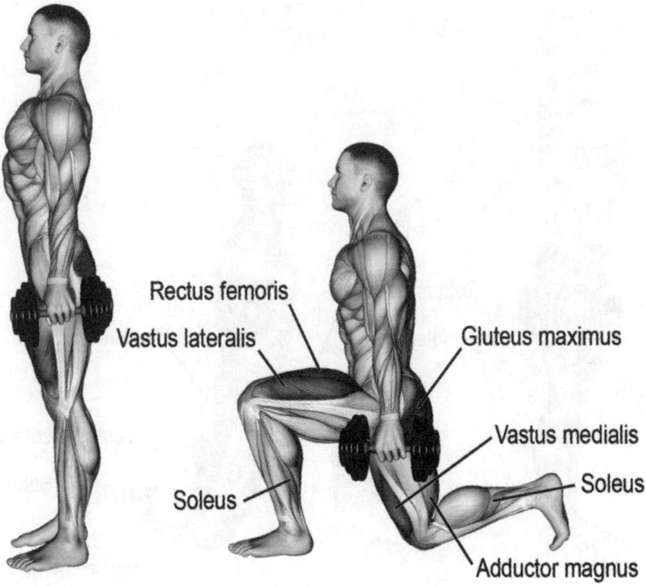

DUMBBELL STANDING LUNGE
4 SETS, 12 REPS EACH

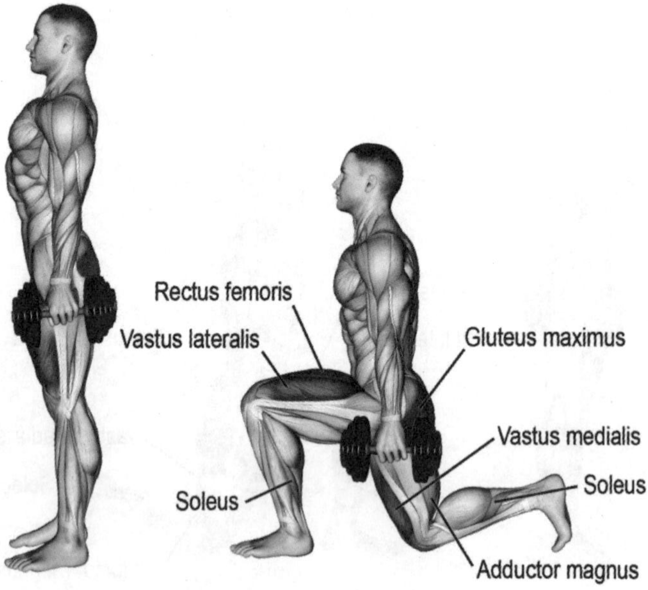

LEG PRESS
4 SETS, 12 REPS EACH

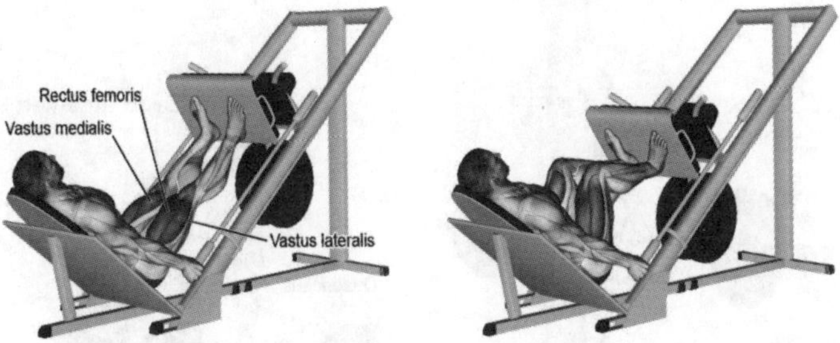

LEG EXTENSION
4 SETS, 12 REPS EACH

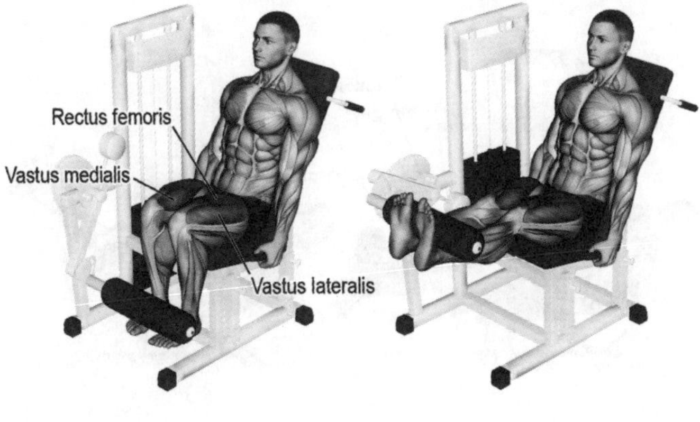

DEAD LIFT
4 SETS, 12 REPS EACH

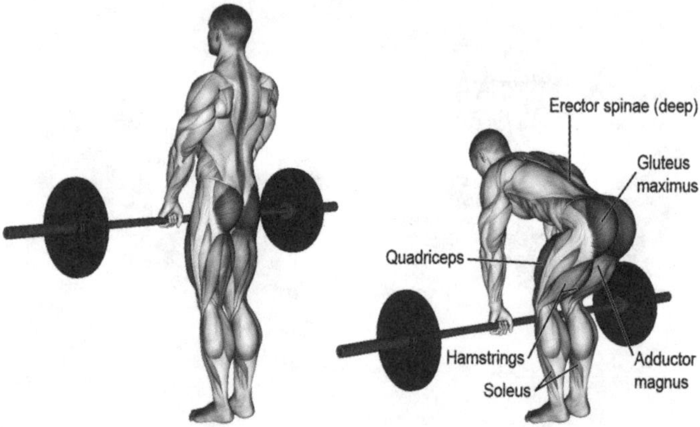

HAMSTRING CURL
4 SETS, 12 REPS EACH

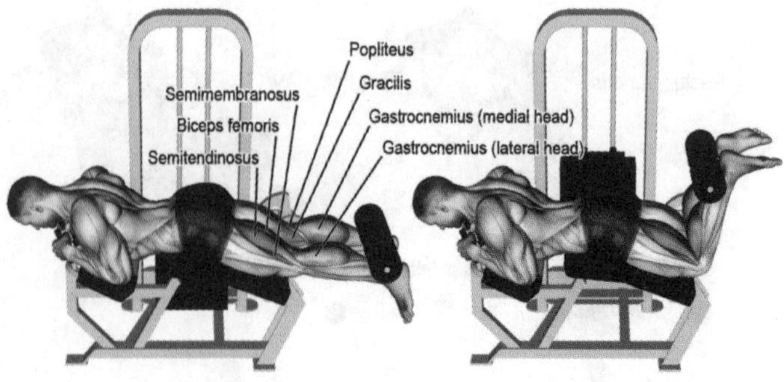

SEATED CALF RAISES
4 SETS, 12 REPS EACH

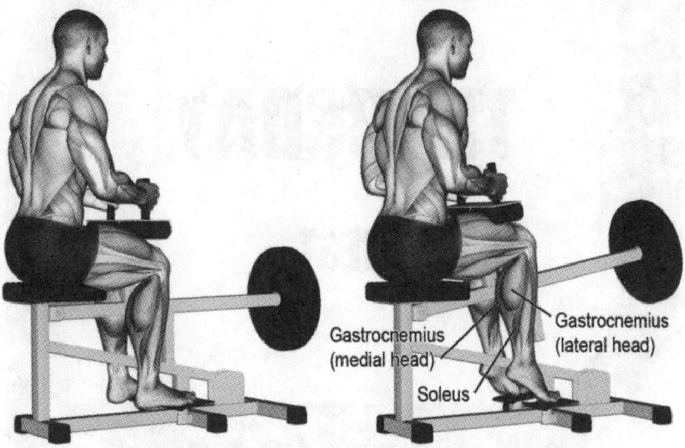

THURSDAY

REST

FRIDAY

REPEAT MONDAY

SATURDAY

REPEAT TUESDAY

SUNDAY

REPEAT WEDNESDAY

WEEK 7 WEEK 8

REPEAT STRENGTH TRAINING

WEEK 9

Monday: Legs

Warm up

10 minutes walking

50 push ups (break it to a set of 3)

50 free squats

MAIN WORKOUT

LEG EXTENSION
4 SETS, 12 REPS EACH

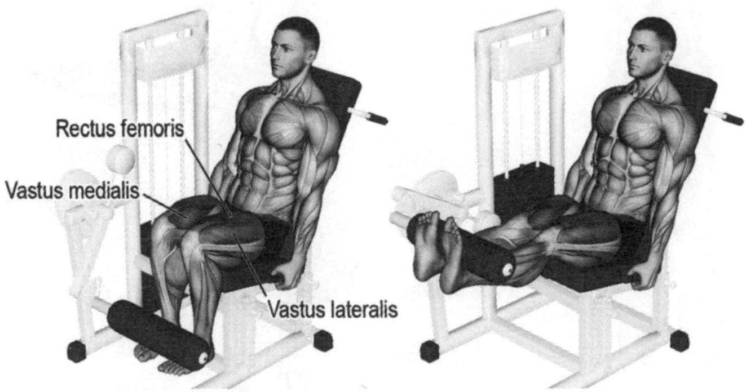

SQUATS
4 SETS, 12 REPS EACH

LEG CURL 4 SETS, 12 REPS EACH

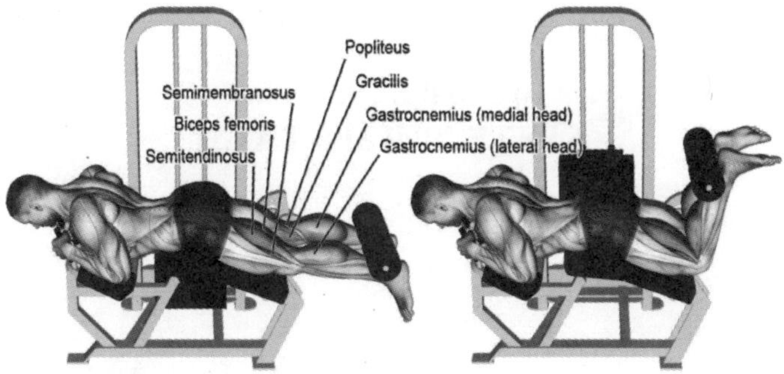

WALKING LUNGES 4 SETS, 12 REPS EACH

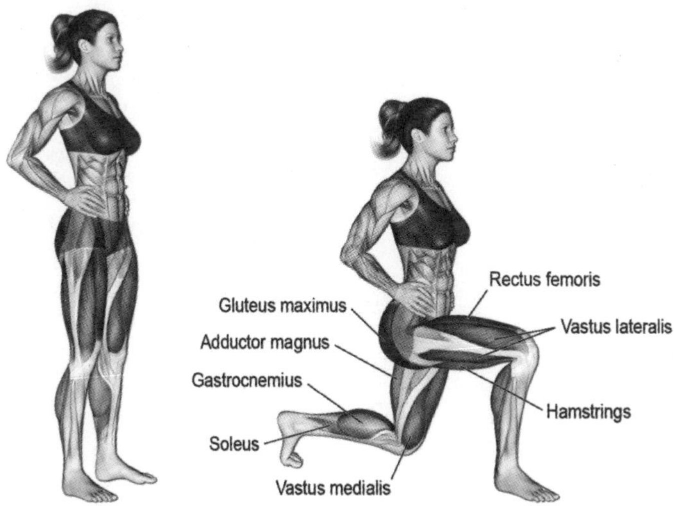

JUMP SQUATS
6 SETS, 10 REPS EACH

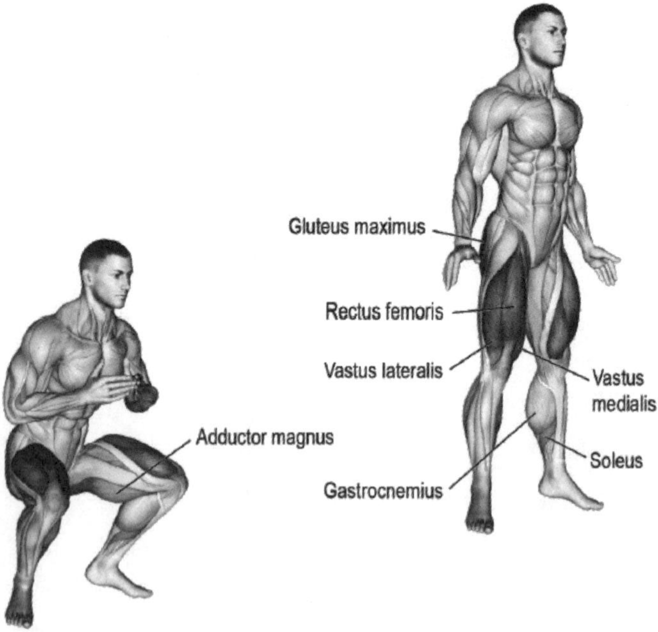

CARDIO

20 MINUTES INCLINE WALK ON TREADMILL

Tuesday: Chest and back

Warm up

10 minutes walking

50 push ups (break it to a set of 3)

MAIN WORK OUT CHEST

FLAT BENCH PRESS 4 SETS 12 REPS EACH

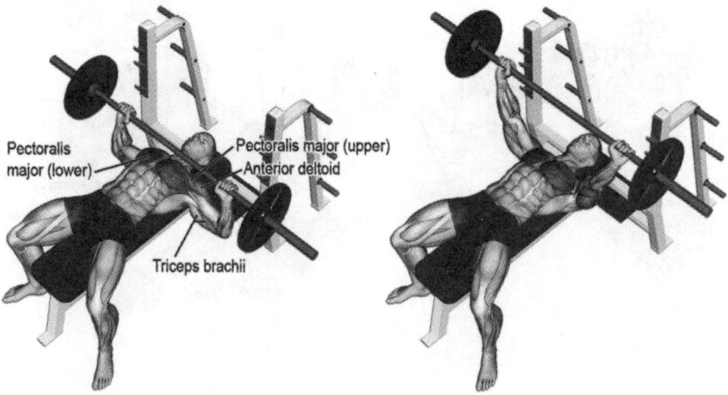

INCLINE DUMBBELL PRESS 4 SETS 12 REPS EACH

FLAT FLY 4 SETS 12 REPS EACH

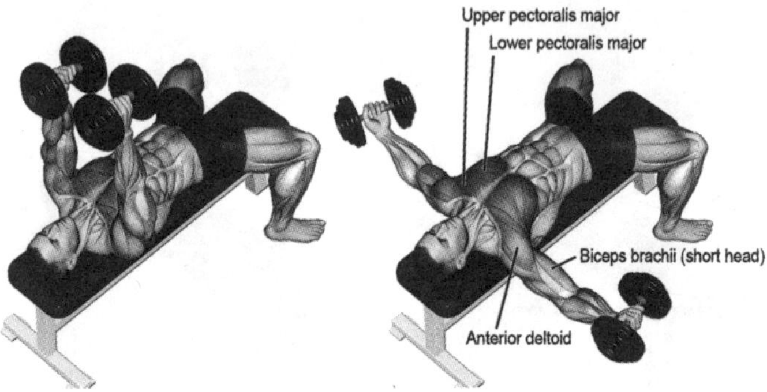

PEC DEC FLY 4 SETS 12 REPS EACH

PULL UPS
4 SETS 12 REPS EACH

LAT PULL DOWN
4 SETS 12 REPS EACH

SINGLE ARM DUMBBELL ROW
4 SETS 12 REPS EACH

STANDING T BAR ROWS
4 SETS 12 REPS EACH

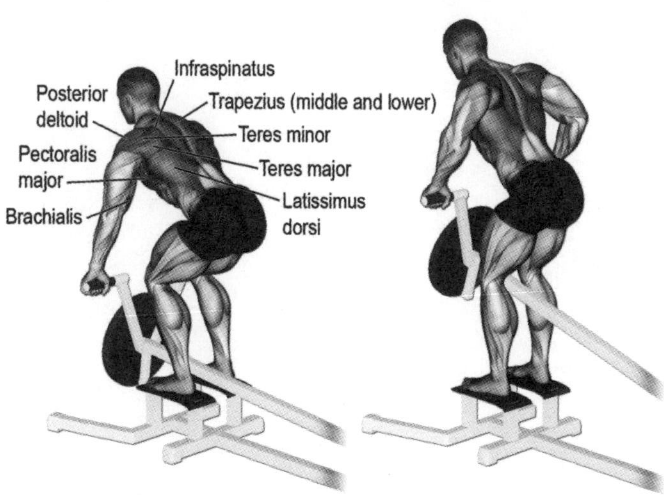

CARDIO
20 MINS INCLINE WALKING

Wednesday: Arms and abs

Warm up

10 minutes walking

50 push ups (break it to a set of 3)

MAIN WORKOUT ARMS

BARBELL CURLS
4 SETS 12 REPS EACH

TRICEP PUSH DOWN
4 SETS 12 REPS EACH

DUMBBELL CURLS
4 SETS 12 REPS EACH

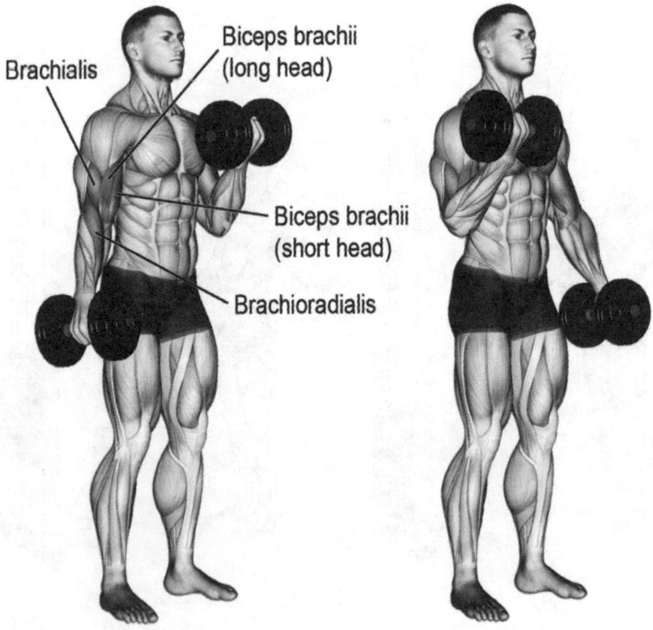

TRICEPS KICK BACKS
4 SETS 12 REPS EACH

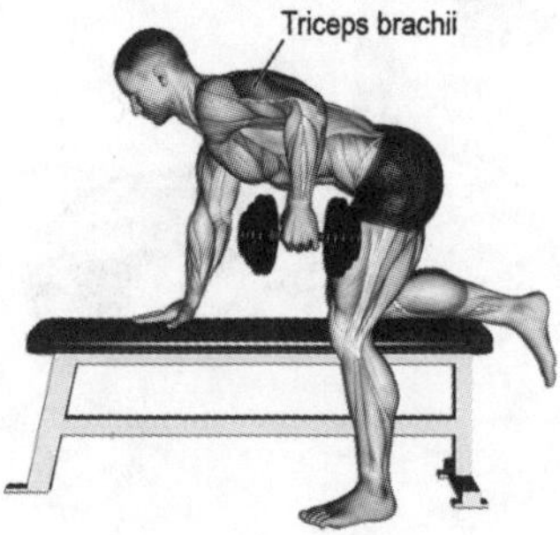

CONCENTRATION CURLS
4 SETS 12 REPS EACH

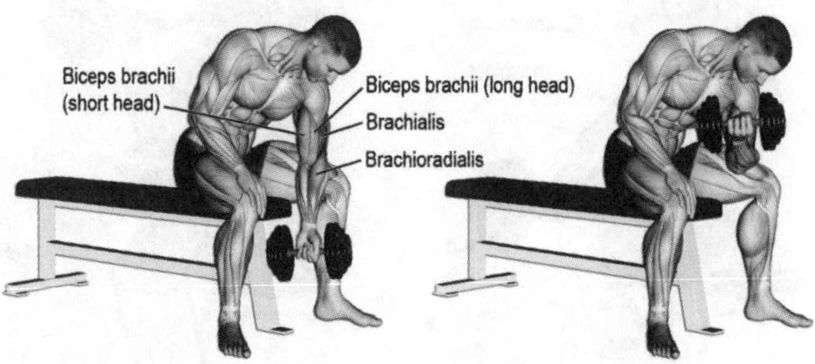

TRICEPS EXTENSION
4 SETS 12 REPS EACH

PREACHER CURLS
4 SETS 12 REPS EACH

TRICEPS DIPS
4 SETS 12 REPS EACH

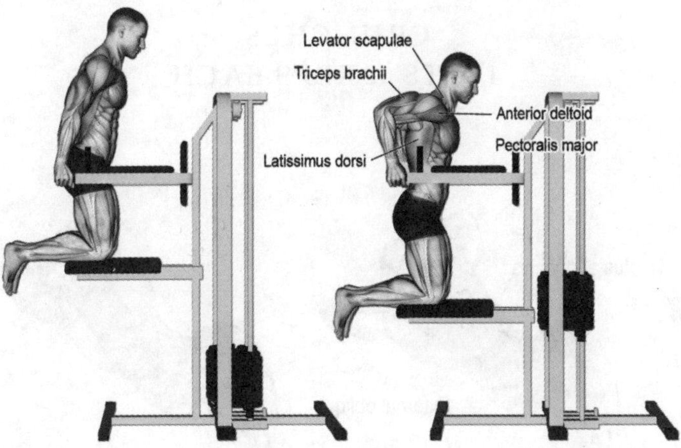

MAIN WORKOUT ABS

CRUNCHES
4 SETS 12 REPS EACH

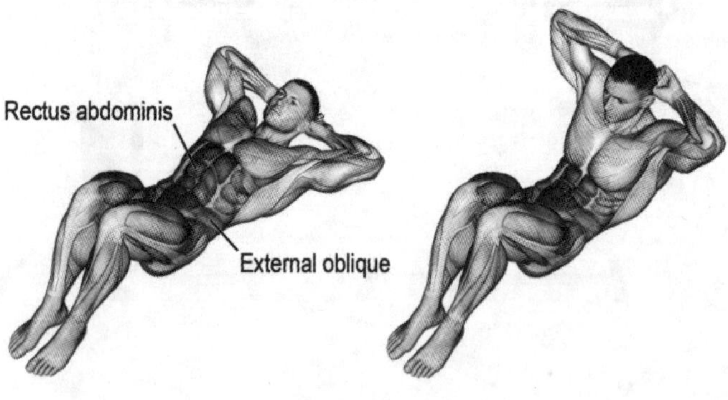

LEG RAISES
4 SETS 12 REPS EACH

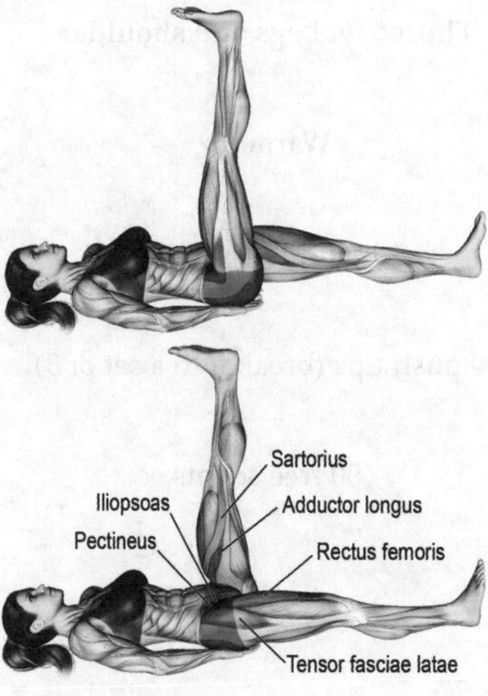

Thursday: Legs and shoulder

Warm up

10 minutes walking

50 push ups (break it to a set of 3)

50 free squats

LEGS WORKOUT

LEG EXTENSION
4 SETS, 12 REPS EACH

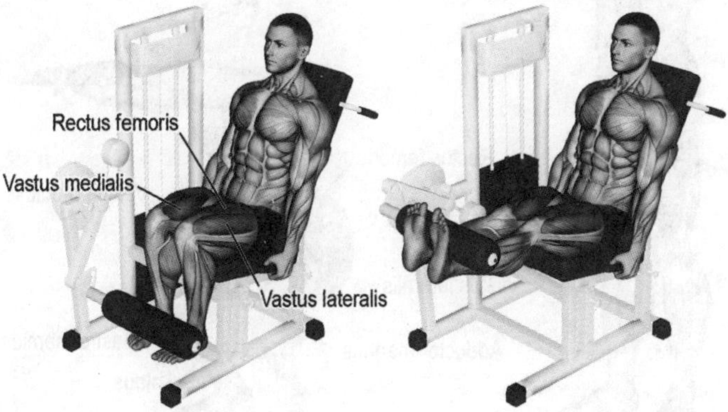

SQUATS
4 SETS, 12 REPS EACH

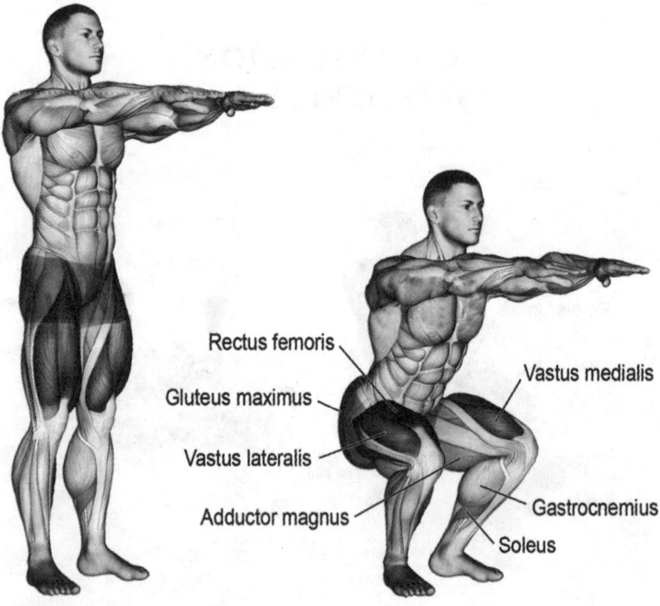

LEG CURL
4 SETS, 12 REPS EACH

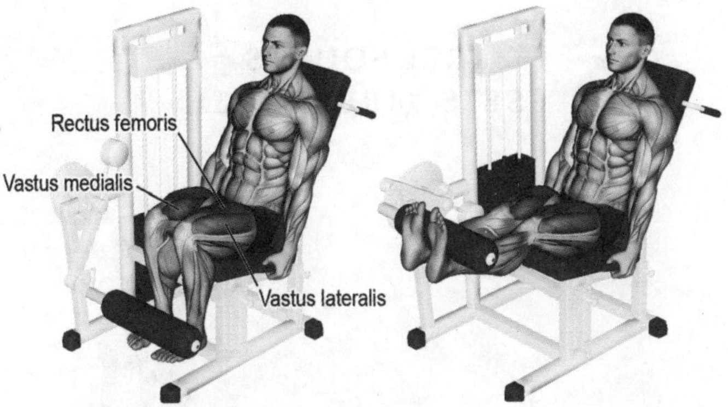

WALKING LUNGES
4 SETS, 12 REPS EACH

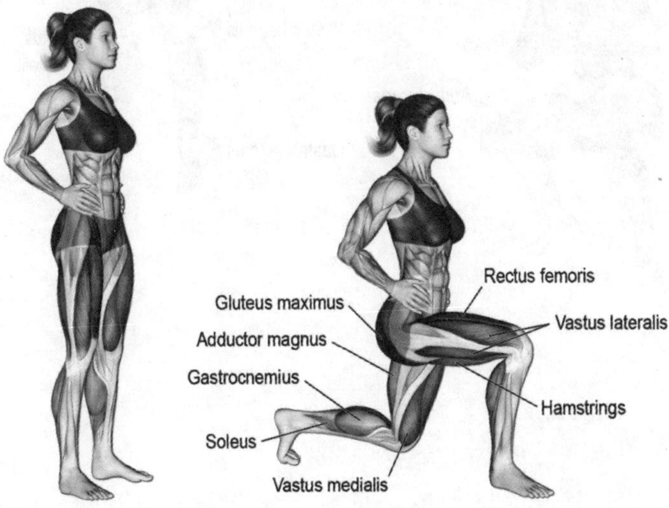

FREE SQUATS
6 SETS, 10 REPS EACH

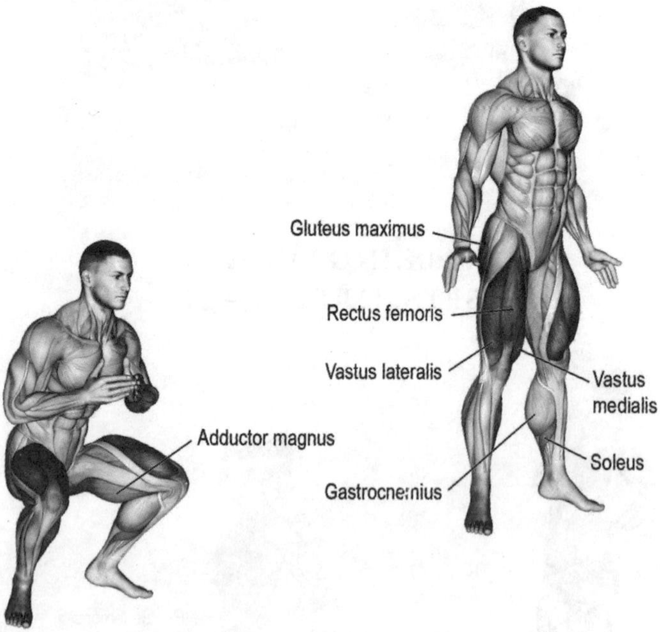

WORKOUT SHOULDERS

SHOULDER DUMBBELL PRESS
4 SETS, 12 REPS EACH

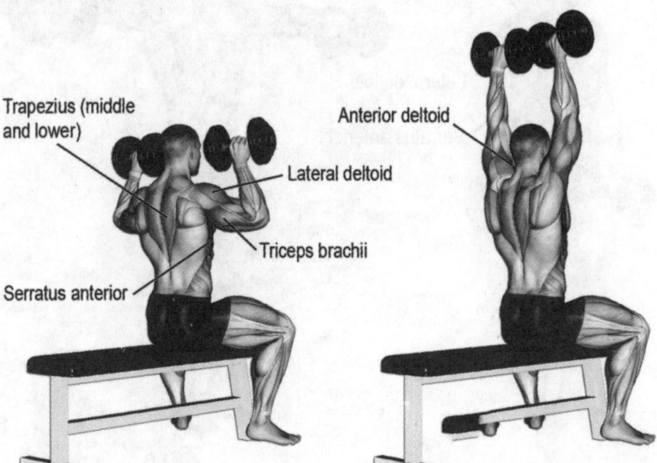

SIDE LATERALS
4 SETS, 12 REPS EACH

FRONT RAISES
4 SETS, 12 REPS EACH

SHRUGS
4 SETS, 12 REPS EACH

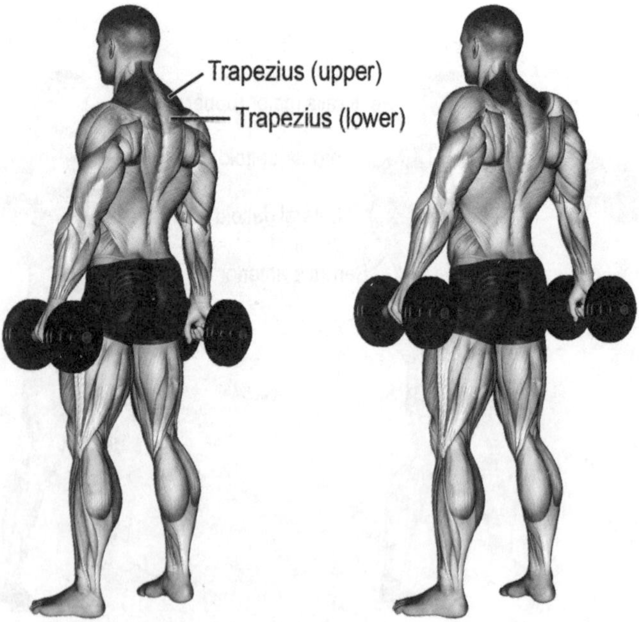

CARDIO
15 MINS WALKING

FRIDAY

REPEAT TUESDAY

SATURDAY

REPEAT WEDNESDAY

SUNDAY

REST

WEEK 10

BODY WEIGHT TRAINING

Super set, with 25-second rest in between each exercise.

6 exercises makes one set, total we do 6 sets total 36 sets per work out.

Monday, Wednesday and Friday- three days work out

MONDAY

EXERCISE 1
PUSH UPS – 25 REPS

EXERCISE 2
FREE SQUATS- 25 REPS

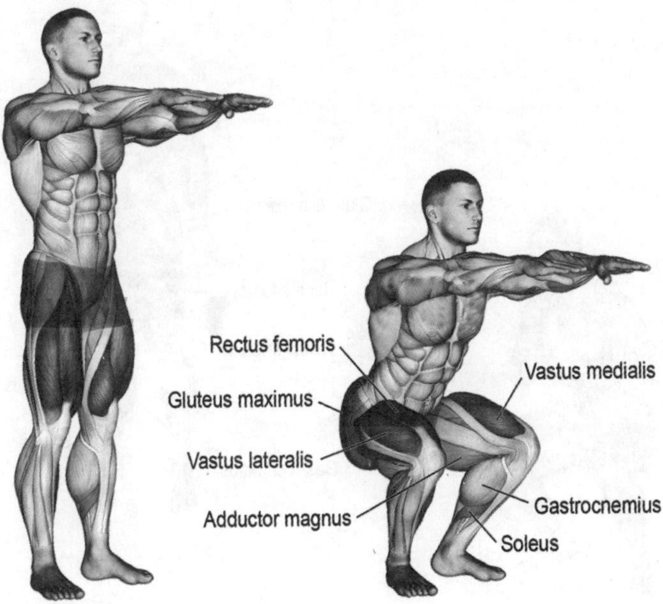

EXERCISE 3
JUMPING JACKS- 25 REPS

EXERCISE 4
LUNGES- 25 REPS

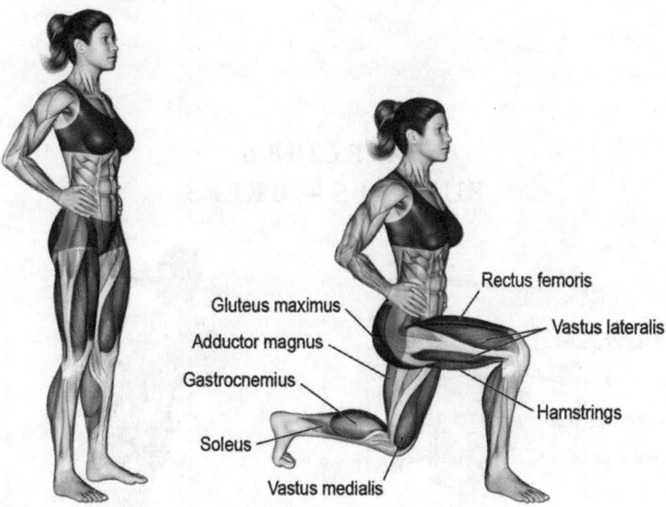

EXERCISE 5
PLANK – TWO MINUTE HOLD

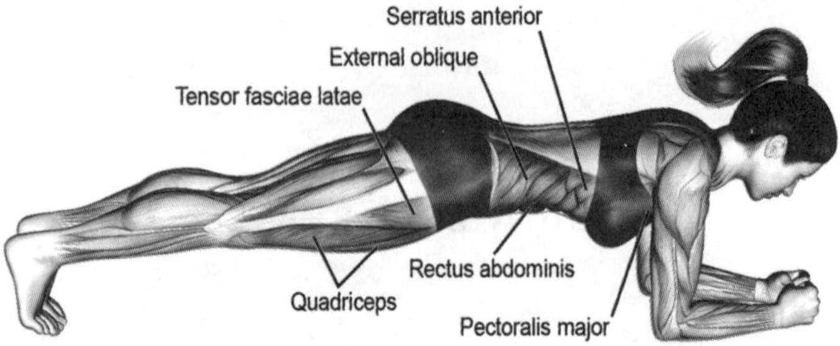

EXERCISE 6
PULL UPS – 20 REPS

WEEK 11 AND 12

Monday

Target area: Legs

Warm up

10 minutes walking

50 push ups (break it to a set of 3)

50 free squats

MAIN WORKOUT

LEG EXTENSION
4 SETS, 12 REPS EACH

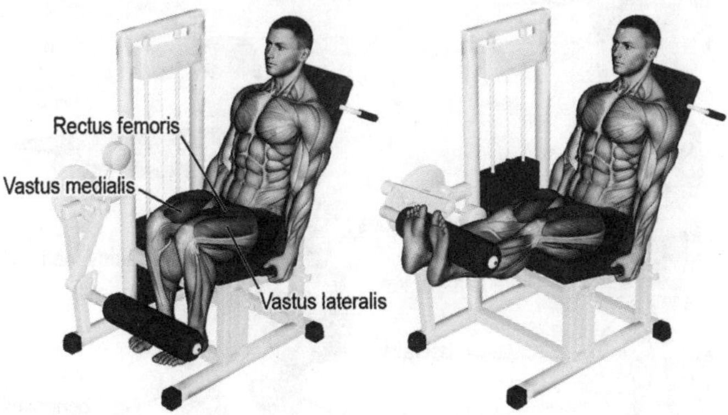

SQUATS
4 SETS, 12 REPS EACH

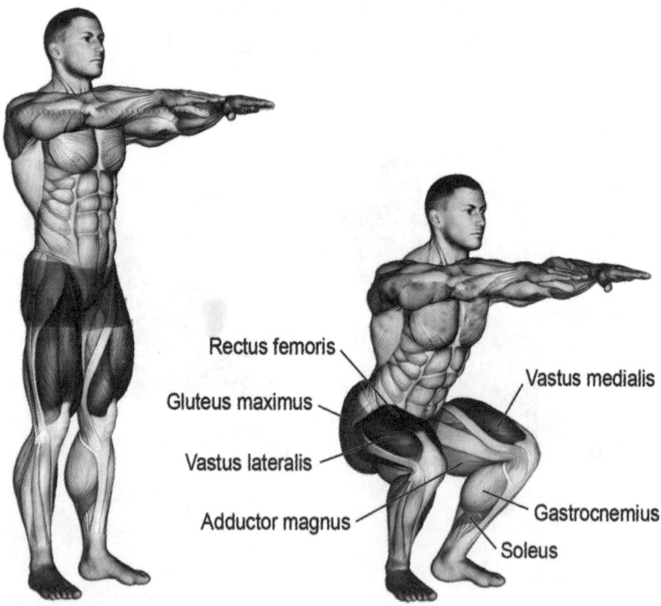

LEG CURL
4 SETS, 12 REPS EACH

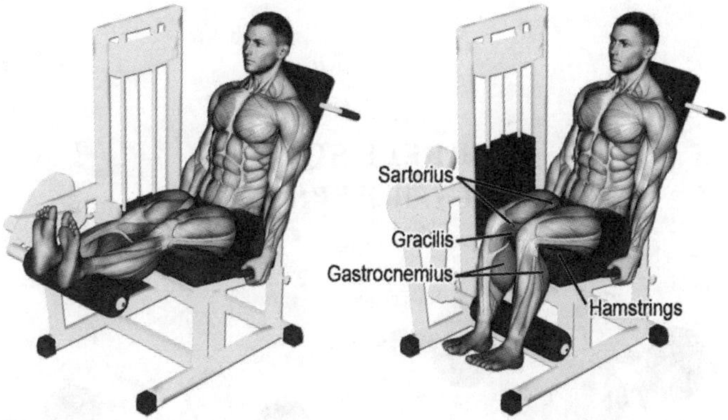

WALKING LUNGES
4 SETS, 12 REPS EACH

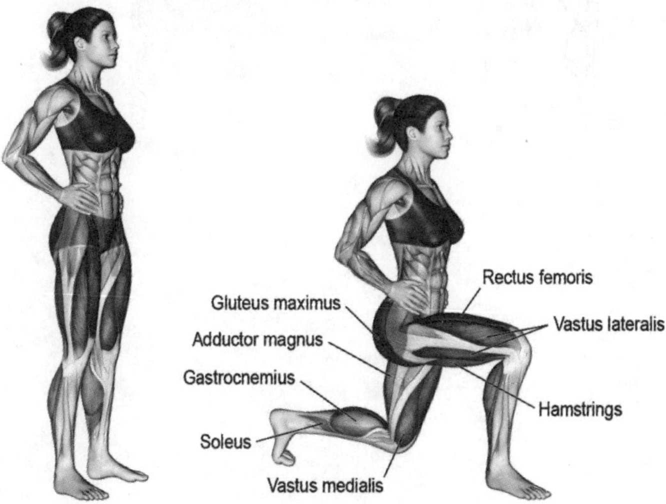

BARBELL SQUATS
6 SETS, 10 REPS EACH

CARDIO

20 MINUTES INCLINE WALK ON TREADMILL

Tuesday

Target area: Chest and back

Warm up

10 minutes walking

50 push ups (break it to a set of 3)

WORKOUT CHEST

FLAT BENCH PRESS
4 SETS 12 REPS EACH

INCLINE DUMBBELL PRESS
4 SETS 12 REPS EACH

FLAT FLY
4 SETS 12 REPS EACH

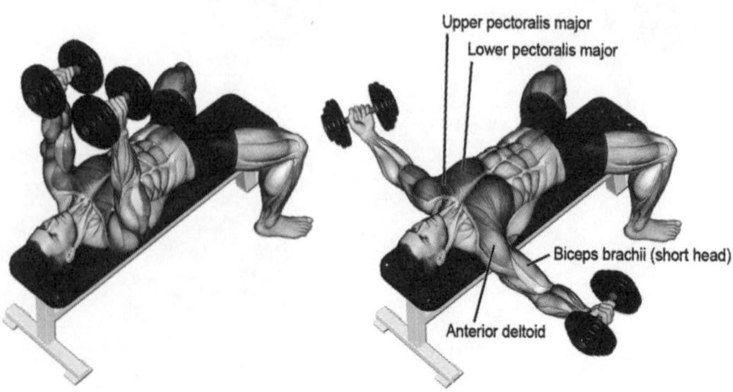

PEC DEC FLY
4 SETS 12 REPS EACH

PULL UPS
4 SETS 12 REPS EACH

LAT PULL DOWN
4 SETS 12 REPS EACH

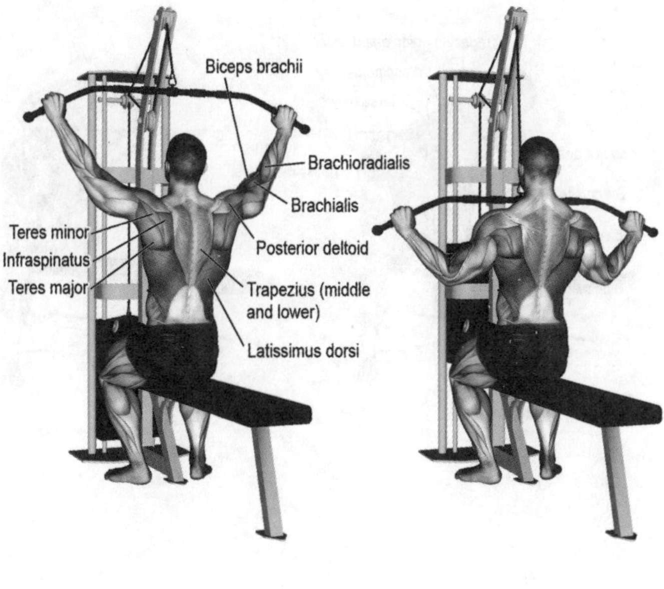

SINGLE ARM DUMBBELL ROW
4 SETS 12 REPS EACH

STANDING T BAR ROWS
4 SETS 12 REPS EACH

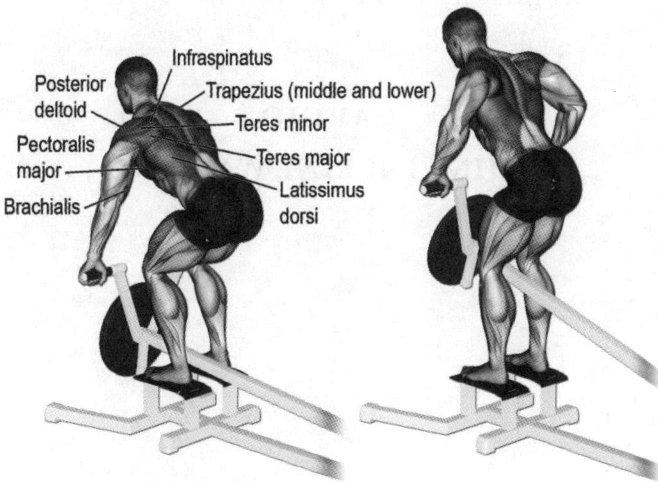

CARDIO
20 MINS INCLINE WALKING

Wednesday

Target area: Arms and abs

Warm up

10 minutes walking

50 push ups (break it to a set of 3)

MAIN WORKOUT ARMS

BARBELL CURLS
4 SETS 12 REPS EACH

TRICEP PUSH DOWN
4 SETS 12 REPS EACH

DUMBBELL CURLS
4 SETS 12 REPS EACH

TRICEPS KICK BACKS
4 SETS 12 REPS EACH

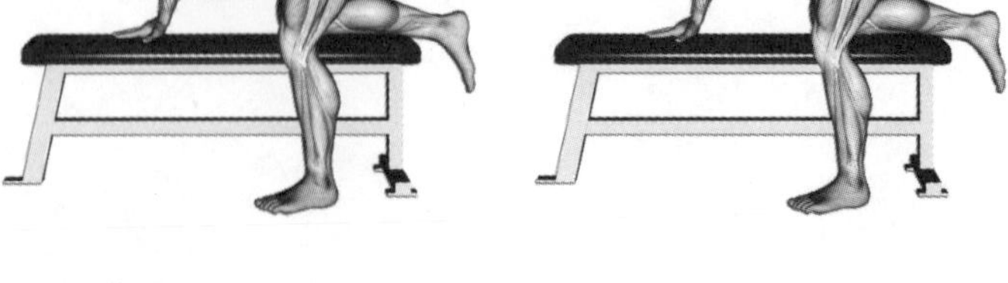

CONCENTRATION CURLS
4 SETS 12 REPS EACH

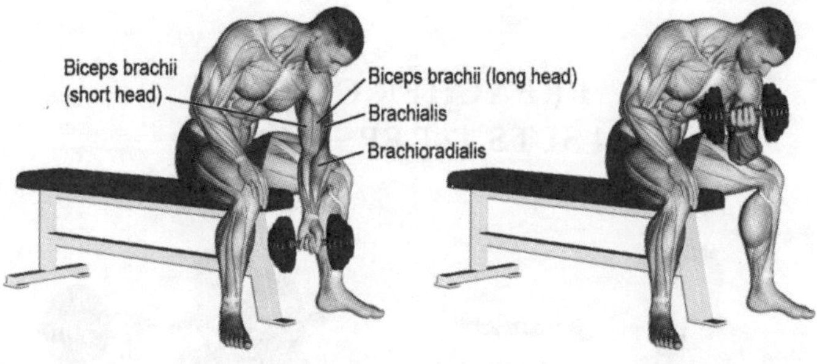

TRICEPS EXTENSION
4 SETS 12 REPS EACH

PREACHER CURLS
4 SETS 12 REPS EACH

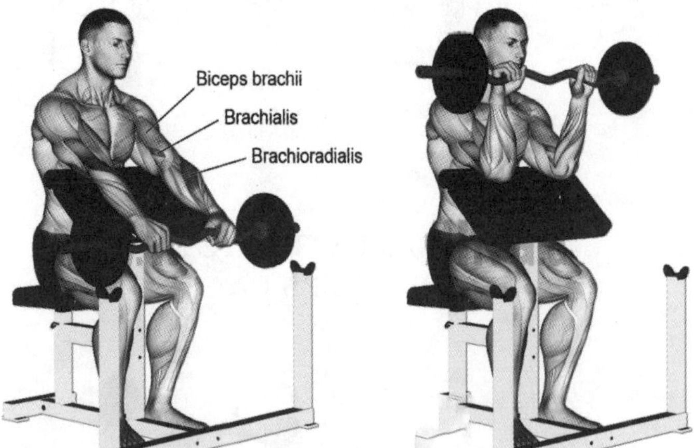

TRICEPS DIPS
4 SETS 12 REPS EACH

MAIN WORKOUT ABS

CRUNCHES
4 SETS 12 REPS EACH

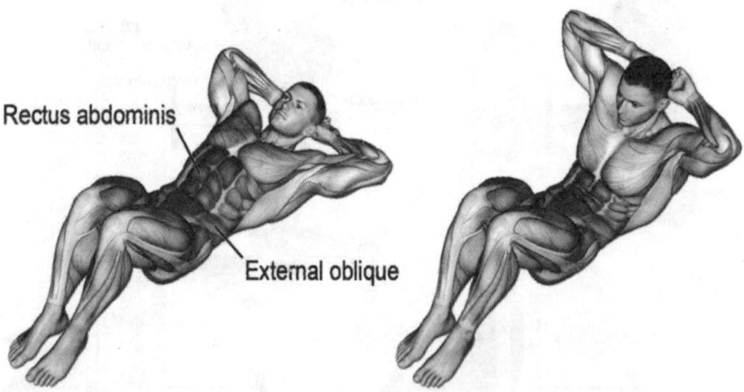

LEG RAISES
4 SETS 12 REPS EACH

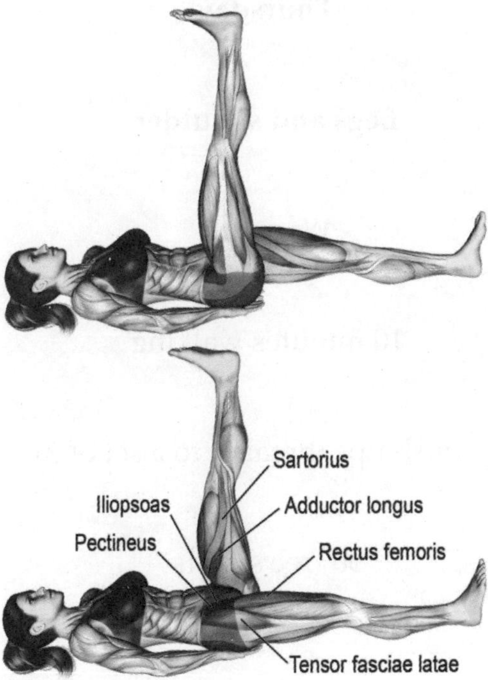

Thursday

Legs and shoulder

Warm up

10 minutes walking

50 push ups (break it to a set of 3)

50 free squats

MAIN WORKOUT LEGS

LEG EXTENSION
4 SETS, 12 REPS EACH

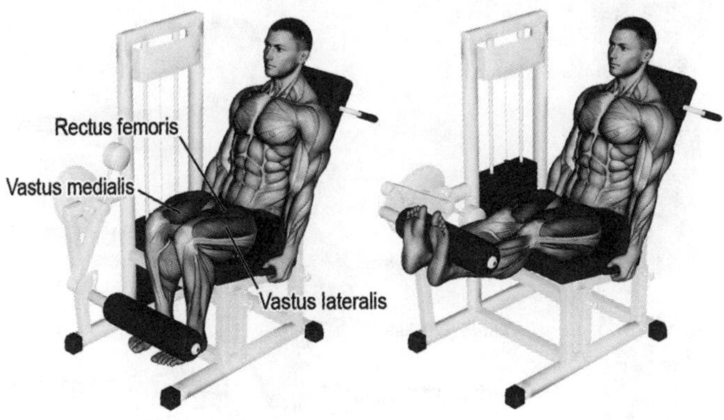

SQUATS
4 SETS, 12 REPS EACH

LEG CURL
4 SETS, 12 REPS EACH

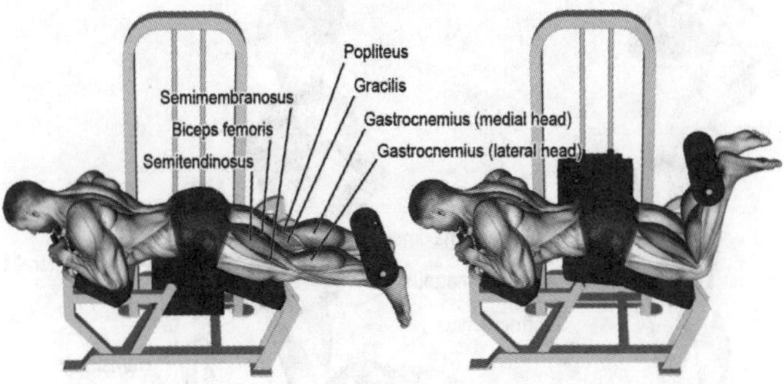

WALKING LUNGES
4 SETS, 12 REPS EACH

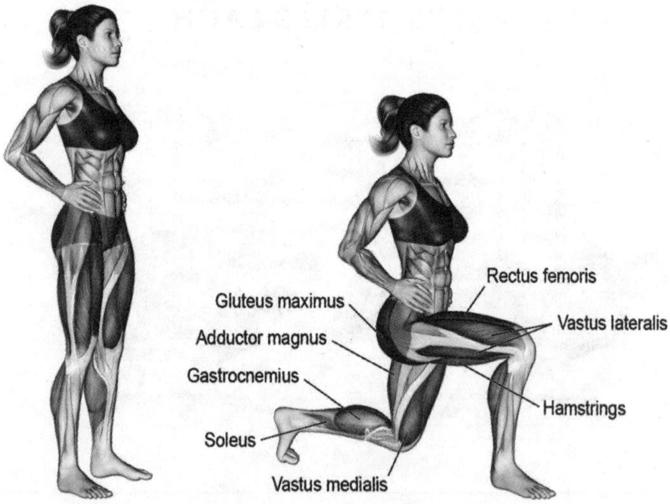

FREE SQUATS
6 SETS, 10 REPS EACH

MAIN WORKOUT SHOULDERS

SHOULDER DUMBBELL PRESS
4 SETS, 12 REPS EACH

SIDE LATERALS
4 SETS, 12 REPS EACH

FRONT RAISES
4 SETS, 12 REPS EACH

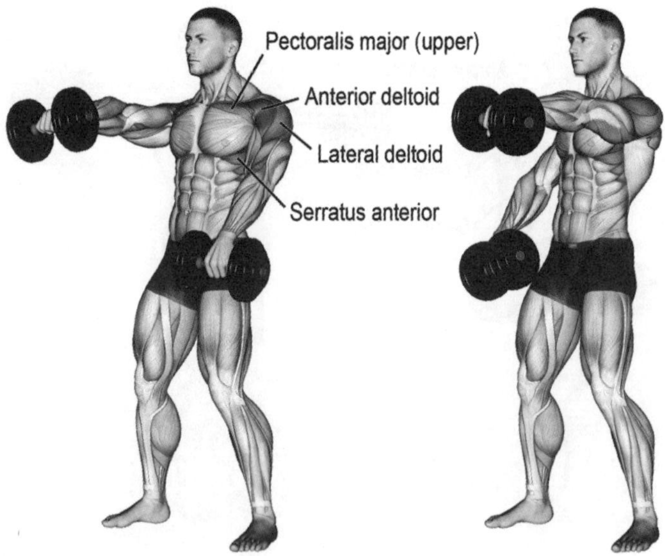

SHRUGS
4 SETS, 12 REPS EACH

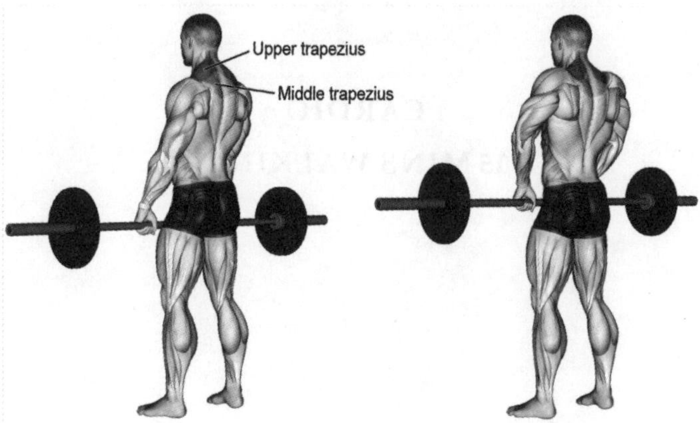

CARDIO
15 MINS WALKING

FRIDAY

REPEAT TUESDAY

SATURDAY

REPEAT WEDNESDAY

SUNDAY

REST

DIET FOR SIX PACK ABS

For this program, we would not tweak our diet too much. The only change you would see will in the workouts and training patterns. The idea is to shock the body, which we will continue via our workouts.

Here is a diet, which you will follow for the next 12 weeks. Please note this is not a fancy diet, but a simple diet plan to stick for weeks. Given the nature of this program, high protein, moderate carbs and fats will bring you tremendous results.

Breakfast

Oats

4 egg whites

10 almonds (soaked)

Post Work Out

1 Scoop whey protein

4 egg whites

sautéed veggies including broccolis, green peppers and lettuce.

Post breakfast snack

1 apple

1 fat free yogurt (100 grams)

Lunch

2 rotis

Grilled chicken/Grilled paneer (200 grams)

Broccoli and spinach (as much as you can)

Post lunch

One orange

10 soaked almonds

Evening snack

1 scoop whey protein

100 grams fat free yogurt

Dinner

250 grams grilled chicken/fish/paneer

Broccoli, spinach and avocados

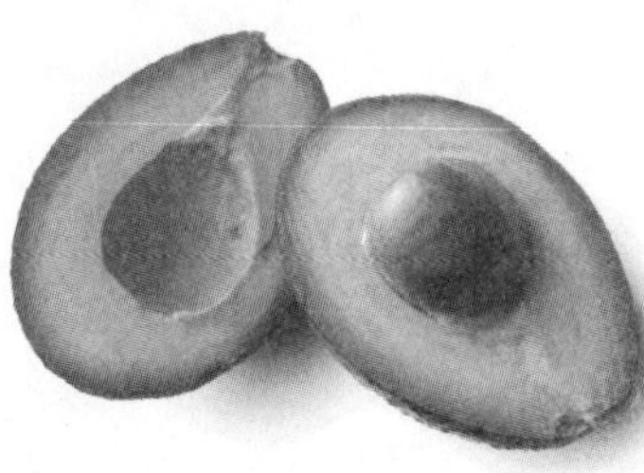

- Whenever hungry eat veggies
- Whenever feel like drinking something, drink coffee (black)
- Don't take too many artificial sweetners.
- Cheat meal every Saturday lunch meal.

HOW TO MAKE 2 LACS A MONTH IN THE FITNESS INDUSTRY

The fitness industry

Fitness industry, lets face it, is not mainstream!

Still it is not considered to be the go to profession when it comes to either making money or for stability. How many times your parents tell you to study for fitness certifications so you could become the best fitness trainer in the country.

I wish they do, but most of them don't!

Actually it is not their fault. Lets be real, what are the career options for you to have a flourishing future in the fitness industry.

1. Become a fitness trainer
2. Become a nutritionist
3. Open up a gym
4. Sell supplements online/retail

But luckily with the new social media boom, the new engagement platform has opened up which is helping lot many fitness enthusiasts make a decent living off their skill. What are those new avenues-

1. Online trainer
2. Youtuber
3. Influencer
4. Sponsored athlete

Lets look at each one in detail

I will keep the content of this book to the point, so that you get to implement most of it without wasting any time reading.

Career secret- developing passive income

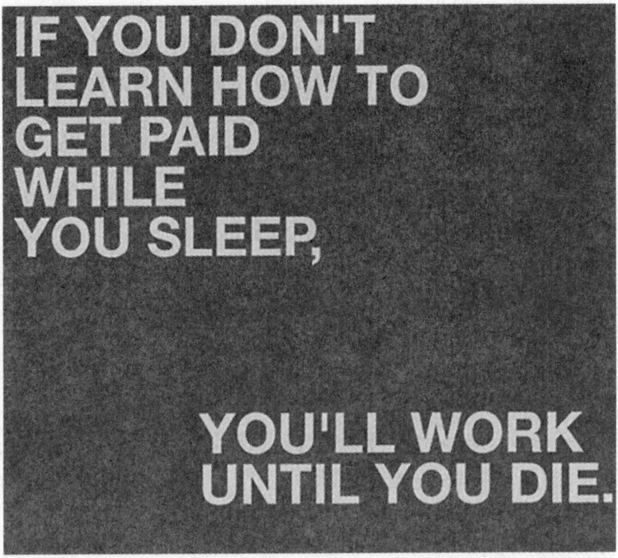

I have to share this secret with you. Whatever you want to do in any industry regardless of fitness, you have to know one thing. Which is this -

Focus as much time in generating passive income for you, not active income. Someone who doesn't understand this, let me simplify it

When you are doing a 9-5 job weather working in a gym or an office, you will get paid by the number of hours you spend in the workplace, which is also called your monthly salary. Even if you spend one hour extra, chances are there would not be any overtime, well most of the times.

This is what active income is. You will only get paid an X amount no matter how hard you try. The biggest drawback of active income is that if you leave your job or fall sick, your money will get deducted from your salary. For you to be making money you need to be active and go to office every frigging day. This is what 95% of the people are doing.

Now lets talk about the 5% of people who have cracked the passive income code.

Now imagine you don't have to go to any office, you work from home or any part of the world without having a boss. Yes I am serious, it is possible!

Here is how passive income works.

You create a YouTube video and it starts getting numerous views! And with every view, YouTube pays you in whichever part of the world you are from or living. You only put in the effort once, to create a video and then you get recurring income from that video every month.

Here is another one!

After seeing that video you created, various brands reaches out to you to promote their products. For example, if you did a viral fitness video, a supplement company will reach out to you to review their product and guess what they will pay you for your review.

You can create your videos anywhere at your own will and not just YouTube but also the brands pay you. This is what the world of passive income looks like.

I am a by-product of passive income. I realized couple of years ago before I left my job of an investment banker and started focusing on opening up streams of passive income for myself.

And I stumbled upon YouTube. And by God's grace and people's love I was India's first full time fitness you tuber, means I made money from making videos for YouTube. Sounds insane, right!

You have got something to think about now

The idea of this book is to have you think differently and how you can get more smarter and make lacs a month. All it takes for you is to focus on passive income.

So now lets discuss, some other passive income streams in the fitness industry. Are you ready.

Online Trainer

Imagine five years ago, what a job of a fitness trainer was!

He would wake up early morning, open up the gym and train clients. And the clients he/she could train were also limited. If I were to go by one hour training session, it means the trainer can only train eight clients in a day, four in the morning and four in the evening.

Now lets see how much money a trainer can make in the conventional model-

If the trainer salary is Rs. 10,000 a month. Over and above, training these eight clients he as per most gym revenue share guidelines will make forty percent of those eight clients.

If the cost of training a client per hour is Rs. 500, training eight clients would mean Rs. 4000/day.

Revenue split of forty percent, the trainer gets, Rs. 1600/day. Plus training clients three days a week. If I were to add up the numbers, the trainer will make Rs. 19200 plus Rs. 10,000 as his monthly salary.

And if trainer falls sick, he will not be paid, the thumb-rule of active income.

Now do you think this is a lucrative career option. You spend hours the whole month to earn approx. Rs. 30,000. Not to forget, he would also have to spend money on his supplements and diet. So he is left with Rs. 15,000 in which he would also have to run the household living and save up apparently.

This is the reason why fitness WAS not a lucrative career option.

But let me reverse it for you by introducing the Online trainer option.

Now, you don't need to go to any gym to train anyone. You only go for your own training. You now, train all your clients online via Instagram or facebook, whatapp, which allows you to train more than eight clients a day. All you do now is just make fitness plans for your clients and charge them.

Lets look at some numbers.

As an online trainer, you are charging Rs. 1000 a month from clients to help them with their diet and training. You don't have to physically train them. The amount of time you take to create their fitness plan is thirty minutes a week to change their plans every week. You are technically spending four hours per client/month.

Seeing great results, these clients have recommended you to their friends and family and now you have over fifty clients and you are generating over Rs. 50,000 a month just by sitting at home.

Read the numbers now

As a gym trainer–You are spending

- 10 hours/day
- Six days a week
- 240 hours a month (60*4)
- For 8 clients
- To earn Rs. 30,000

As a online trainer – You are spending

- Two hours/client/month
- 100 hours a month
- For 50 clients
- To earn Rs. 50,000

Now you tell me, what would you do.

As a trainer, you need to get smart! Move away from the conventional style of generating revenue/ money. The world has changed and is changing every day. Get used to it or be obsolete like earning Rs. 30000 a month for spending endless hours in a place, which wont even value you.

Youtuber

This is my personal favorite.

You can be both online trainer and a you tuber, which means income from every frigging source. Now lets take an example of the same gym trainer who is working in a gym. All he is doing is telling his clients the proper movement and weight lifting techniques for which he is being paid his salary and personal training incentives (remember 40%)

Now if he is smart, which I am sure he will get after reading this book, all he can do is make a video of the correct movement, which he is telling his clients. But this time his client is YouTube and all the millions of people who are watching his video.

People liked his style of teaching weight training movements and subscribed to his channel. These subscribers are also asking him if he could train them, and become their online trainer.

On the other side, YouTube is paying him for subscribers watching his videos (views). He has now doubled his income simply by uploading his training videos. Plus also people in the fitness industry are beginning to take notice of him.

While earlier he was only a small trainer working in a small gym, for peanuts! Now he is connected to millions of people who are waiting to see his next video and some even eagerly waiting to meet him. Simply by uploading a video he has developed a following and is now a social media revolution.

So the question is how much does YouTube pay?

YouTube has a different algorithm for different countries. But a creator with decent following can easily make Rs. 25-35000 a month as his YouTube earnings. Which means YouTube is paying this content creator to make videos. Remember earlier he was making Rs. 30000 for spending hours in the gym training only eight people a month.

This is the power of YouTube.

So don't underestimate it

Influencer

Here is another one.

Again I will take the same example of that gym trainer who was training 8 clients for Rs. 30000 a month. Now he is making money from online training, YouTube videos and if that's not enough brands are also reaching out to him for promotions.

Why are brands reaching out to this trainer?

Simply because he is connected to so many people and his subscribers love his content. Brands also want to leverage that opportunity to promote their brand amongst his followers/subscribers so they could sell their product.

So what do they do, they reach out to this trainer who is now very popular in the fitness industry and they ask him to review their product. And in return the brand is willing to pay a decent amount. Now imagine a trainer who was struggling to make a living is now suddenly approached by big brands to promote their product for insane amount of money.

How much brands usually pay for online promotions

The brand can pay from Rs. 10,000 to Rs. 3 lacs depending on the product and the Youtuber subscriber count. What a classic example of passive income.

Earlier the same trainer was showing his client how to do weight training movement, which is now being replaced with a video of that same movement plus a brand is paying him to integrate their product in that same video.

Congratulations, this trainer has now become a fitness influencer.

Influencer is a social media personality with a huge following who is known amongst masses for his/her content and value add.

Sponsored athlete

This is also an amazing way to generate extra income in the fitness industry.

Lets say a supplement brand reaches out to you to integrate their product in your videos. Which is what you do, as a fitness influencer. They liked you so much that they decided to you make you their athlete/ambassador to promote all their products for a price, which they will pay you monthly.

Now this is insane! Same guy who was a small gym trainer is now a big fitness influencer and is being paid for everything he is doing in the fitness industry plus is endorsing various brands as their athlete or ambassador.

So if were to add up the income stream now what would you get

- Rs. 50,000/month from online training
- Rs. 30,000/month from YouTube
- Rs. 1,00000 as product integrations
- Rs. 50,000 as product endorser

This trainer is now making over Rs. 2 lacs a month. This is the power of passive income and being smart in the fitness industry.

Now all this sound too good to be true, but this all boils down to the action plan which you need to implement if you want to make Rs. 2 lacs a month

Are you ready! Lets go

Action plan to make 2 lacs/month

Have a goal

The problem with most of the people in the fitness industry is that they don't have a concrete goal on how they want to make money. Remember only training people, is not a sustainable or scalable way to grow your personal fitness brand. As a fitness professional, you need to start thinking like an entrepreneur on how you will make not just your money but also make an impact in the fitness industry.

Have a goal, which scares you!

I remember getting into the fitness industry and being criticized by lot many banker friends of mine. They told me I am making the biggest mistake of my life. There is nothing in the fitness industry, how are you going to survive, I remember someone even asking me" what's my survival strategy?

But I knew and was very clear in my head that I don't want to open up a gym or become a trainer, I wanted to do something which everyone can follow later on. This was a noble thought also a steep goal. I not only got into this industry but also became India's leading fitness influencer, Co Founder of a supplement company, and a founder of event company, TG Connect which sponsors needy athletes. Till date, we have sponsored over two hundred needy athletes.

To top it off, John Abraham, Producer and Actor, was the one who officially launched TG connect for me. I only got to know him after getting into the fitness industry.

Point is, if you think big, big things will happen to you and you will end up working with people who are bigger than you in the industry.

Learn to communicate

I come across so many talented fitness trainers who have challenges expressing their thought process. If you can't share what you have in mind, how else the world will know your intent to change the fitness industry.

Learn to express, it could be any language Hindi or English, whichever language you are comfortable in. It's your ability to express, which will attract people to you. Having a good body is not good enough in the fitness industry.

You can see so many people with average physiques but great communication skills are doing so well. Spend the same amount of time in learning to communicate than you spend in your gym training.

Start reading books either on fitness or general. This will keep you relevant in the industry and ensure you know your subject well.

Stay humble

Don't you come across guys who have a great physique but their attitude sucks. They feel they are God gift to human kind. They are super arrogant and looking for ways to pin people down.

You don't have to be like them.

Having a great physique and good manners is a deadly combination, in my opinion, a recipe for success. Don't be arrogant, just because you have a good physique.

Remember physique is very temporary and will not last for long but your attitude will.

Add value

I see so many YouTube channels these days cropping up the scene. But all of them are talking about the same thing. Which is good but how would you differentiate yourself.

The only way to differentiate yourself from others is to add value to people's lives. Create content, which will help people. But what people are doing is creating content, which is making them look good.

Remember it is not about you looking good in the video but what you are sharing with your subscribers.

Looks will get boring, but content will always bring back people.

I remember some of my videos are shot in my living room, with no lighting and a very average camera set up but a very useful topic.

Those videos have fetched me million of views. No one cares about the backdrop or what you wear, so long you are helping them with the information they need.

Be real and honest

I come across so many trainers who are so pseudo, meaning they project a very different image of themselves, which actually they are not.

Remember, social media is not about putting a picture with a pout with an Armani suit, it is about showing the real you. What I mean is, if you want people to connect with you, you have to show them the real you. Not the one who you project yourself to be.

If you see me in real life, I am exactly the same. I don't drive fancy cars, not that I can't afford, it is just that I choose to stay like that. I am a real person who is honest. I built my whole fitness business around honesty. I have had ups and downs, where I have been misunderstood but that comes with the job.

Be consistent

This is one of the most important thing I have learnt on being the social media influencer. You need to put content everyday out there, which will add value to people. Sometimes you will get noticed and sometimes you wont. That is fine. But be consistent.

With consistency you need to be patient. You will not become an Internet sensation overnight. You need to be patient and put in effort and consistency.

Invest in a camera

I cant emphasize the importance of having a camera. To tell you the truth, a DSLR has actually changed my life. I never knew that talking to camera and being real can get you so many views. But don't go overboard in investing in the camera. Remember, focus more on content, if the content is good and camera is also good, it will only create magic.

For that magic to happen, do invest in a DSLR. And you don't need any training to operate. Just have a tripod and set it up where you would like to shoot your videos and rest will happen.

Never rehearse

Again this is one of the biggest mistake people make in making videos or projecting themselves on social media to develop their following. Don't rehearse just be impromptu. Let the real you come out. It is ok to make mistakes and falter. No one is perfect and people will love you for being you. Don't change, remember you are making videos for real people not acting.

ABOUT THE AUTHOR

Tarun Gill is India's leading fitness entrepreneur and an influencer with a following of more than 1 million.

He is also a founder of one of India's biggest fitness media digital platform, TG Talks.

He is a graduate from St. Stephens College, Masters in Journalism from Indian institute of Mass Communication and an MBA in marketing management.

After serving more than 5 fortune hundred companies including Metlife, HSBC, GE, IBM, Tarun took up fitness as a full time career, becoming India's first full time fitness Youtuber.

Tarun is also an Amazon bestselling fitness author and a Founder of TG Connect, India's only fitness social recognition platform endorsed by famous Bollywood a listers. With his reach and network, he was able to launch, India's first fitness TV show called the Indian Fitness League, IFL which was aired on DSport, a Premium Sports Channel by Discovery Sports in the year 2018.